DAVID
COULTHARD

As part of our ongoing market research, we are always pleased to receive comments about our books, suggestions for new titles, or requests for catalogues. Please write to: The Editorial Director, Haynes Publishing, Sparkford, Nr Yeovil, Somerset BA22 7JJ.

DAVID
COULTHARD
In the wheeltracks of legends

JIM DUNN

First published in 1995 as *David Coulthard: The Flying Scotsman*
Second edition (*David Coulthard: In the wheeltracks of legends*) published in 1997

British Library Cataloguing in Publication Data:
A catalogue record for this book is
available from the British Library

ISBN 1 85960 406 4

Library of Congress catalog card no. 97–72865

Published by Haynes Publishing, Sparkford,
Nr Yeovil, Somerset, BA22 7JJ, UK.

Haynes Publishing Inc., 861 Lawrence Drive,
Newbury Park, California 91320, USA.

Designed & typeset by G&M, Raunds, Northamptonshire
Printed and bound in France by Imprimerie Pollina s.a., Luçon, France n° 72409

Contents

Acknowledgements   6
Straight from the grid   7

CHAPTER ONE: Scotland's Young Pretender   15

CHAPTER TWO: A small village with big ambitions   22

CHAPTER THREE: Cold as hell but fast as fury   35

CHAPTER FOUR: Young Pretender meets Old Master   47

CHAPTER FIVE: Wheel to wheel with the boss   61

CHAPTER SIX: The first day in May   73

CHAPTER SEVEN: The difference between winning and losing   82

CHAPTER EIGHT: Sometimes coming second can be enough   101

CHAPTER NINE: The new boy makes his mark   113

CHAPTER TEN: Countdown to victory   130

CHAPTER ELEVEN: New team, new problems   147

Appendix: David Coulthard's career highlights   158

Acknowledgements

I WOULD LIKE to thank the Scottish karting and motor racing community, past and present, for all the fun I've had, as well as all the help with this book. Thanks, in no particular order, to Allan McNish, Mark Gallagher, Brian Smith, David Cawthorne, Tom McLaren, Robert Logan, Duncan and Joyce Coulthard, Derek Butcher, Paul and Mark and Jackie Stewart, DC himself, and David Leslie junior, who is perhaps the most frank and honest racing driver I have ever encountered.

Thanks also to *Karting* magazine, *Motoring News*, and *The Scotsman*, whose archives, collectively, carefully chart the career of David Coulthard – and to David Hayhoe, author of *The Grand Prix Data Book*, for verifying statistics. Finally, thanks to Hugh Hunston with whom I shared the excitement of DC's early career, the horror of the first day of May 1994, and David's first few Grands Prix, until my once bitter rival decided to change careers and leave me to follow 'The boy', as we always called him, on my own.

The illustrations are from LAT Photographic except where stated otherwise.

Straight from the grid

WHEN DAVID COULTHARD accelerated his silver McLaren Mercedes along the Melbourne pit straight for the 58th time on Sunday 9 March 1997 he did something he had never done in a car before, something that Formula 1 drivers, the ultimate gladiators in this most macho sport, are not supposed to do. He began to cry.

One lap later, his vision blurred by tears, he angled the car across the finishing line to where team owner Ron Dennis was standing, quite damp-eyed himself. The flying Scot had just broken a drought of three seasons without a victory for the once dominant McLaren team. This was a dream result for the driver, for the team, and for West, their new sponsors. Indeed it was a glittering debut for West, who had signed a five-year deal worth an estimated £64 million, following Marlboro's departure to Ferrari after a 23-year sponsorship deal with McLaren – the most successful partnership in grand prix history – which had yielded 96 race victories, nine drivers' and seven constructors' titles for the distinctive red and white cars.

Mercedes were happy too. This was the German carmaker's first F1 victory since Juan Manuel Fangio won the Italian Grand Prix in 1955 and the third of five World Championships. Thanks largely to the Argentinian's brilliance, Mercedes were used to success. Even after a gap of 38 years, when they rejoined Formula 1 in 1993 – as engine suppliers first to Sauber, then to McLaren – they expected not only to

Overleaf Australia's three times World Champion Sir Jack Brabham waves the chequered flag as David Coulthard crosses the line to win the 1997 Australian Grand Prix, McLaren's first win after a 50-race drought (Popperfoto/Reuter).

win but to dominate the sport. Coulthard's win, in a car sporting the legendary colours of the Mercedes Silver Arrows team, marked their return in style.

So, all in all the Scot's maiden victory for the team in the opening round of the 1997 World Championship season was highly significant.

Coulthard – widely expected to be the top British driver for 1997 – said this win was even better than his first victory, with Williams in 1995, because it was so unexpected. 'It gives everyone in the team a real momentum.'

Coulthard had started the race with no greater ambition than wanting to challenge Michael Schumacher in the Ferrari for third spot on the podium behind the Williams Renault duo of Jacques Villeneuve and Heinz-Harald Frentzen. Villeneuve, who had taken over Coulthard's place at Williams a year previously and gone on to give Damon Hill a real fight for the 1996 crown, was runaway favourite to add the 1997 F1 championship to his 1995 IndyCar title. With Hill's move to Arrows, Villeneuve was the best driver in the best car by a country mile. A country mile in terms of the 1997 Australian Grand Prix translated into a qualifying lap nearly two seconds ahead of everyone else at 1 min 29.369 seconds.

Leading the best of the rest on the front row was Heinz-Harald Frentzen, the man tipped to outpace Michael Schumacher. In the second Williams Renault, Frentzen could only manage 1.31.123. Michael Schumacher, the gifted double World Champion, had wrestled his Ferrari into third position with 1.31.472. Coulthard had somehow got the new McLaren car into fourth spot, a tenth of a second behind the German. Fifth fastest was Eddie Irvine in the second Ferrari. Alongside him on the third row of the grid was Mika Hakkinen in the second McLaren, a full half second behind his team-mate.

The first corner of a race is where all the action happens, and so it proved. Villeneuve fluffed the start allowing Frentzen to get away first. Schumacher too hesitated. Coulthard nosed ahead as they accelerated to 100mph in four seconds and on to nearly double this speed before starting the 190-mile sequence of braking, turning, accelerating. But behind Coulthard both Irvine and Sauber driver Johnny Herbert had made even better starts and engulfed Schumacher and Coulthard in the braking zone for the first corner. Afterwards, everyone blamed Eddie Irvine. They invariably do. The Ulsterman's car hit Villeneuve's

Moving moment. Coulthard waves the Scottish flag from the pit wall, watched by team-mate Mika Hakkinen (Popperfoto/Reuter).

which in turn T-boned Herbert's as he tried to lunge round the outside.

Coulthard, coming hard in fifth spot, braked, just missed Irvine, then found a clear track with only Frentzen ahead. He was in second place as he took the second corner. But behind him, so close that the gap could only be measured in precious hundredths of a second, was bad news. The worst possible news. Michael Schumacher. History records that when Michael Schumacher gets that close to the car in front he also gets past. It was, everyone thought, just a matter of time.

Frentzen, not surprisingly given the superiority of the Williams, began to just drive away. By lap ten he had a 10.5 seconds advantage and could begin to ease up for a tactical drive to the finish and the maiden victory which, with his team-mate gone, was assuredly his.

But it was not that simple. Williams had decided on a two-stop strategy for fuel and tyres. McLaren were going for one. Any loss of speed from running a heavier fuel load and older tyres would be out-balanced over the race distance, they reasoned, by time saved in the pits.

Another less obvious factor was also at play. Heinz-Harald was leading, but had never won, a Grand Prix. These are two very different things – especially if you are already trying to withstand the media pressures of being the golden boy/wicked interloper who replaced Hill at Williams. On lap 18 when he peeled into the pits for his first fuel stop Frentzen was 17.5 seconds ahead of the Scot who, in turn, was just one second clear of Schumacher.

A dozen laps later, nearing half distance, Schumacher gambled on an early stop, hoping he could pass Coulthard when he was pitting. He couldn't and two laps later, when the race had settled, Frentzen was over 18 seconds clear of the Scot and the German, who were still just one second apart and tied, as if by string. The Williams driver began to reel off a series of fastest laps to stretch his lead and allow him to get into and out of the pits for his second and final stop ahead of Coulthard.

When he came in, on lap 40, he had a 23 second lead. It was not quite enough. A sticking rear wheel nut added eight seconds to the time the car was stopped. Coulthard slipped into the lead. Schumacher, just a heartbeat behind him, was into second. HH, sensing he had somehow managed to throw away the race that was only his to lose, stormed out onto the circuit and really turned on the pace.

With Schumacher still one second behind Coulthard, and Frentzen bearing down on his fellow German, everything looked set for one of the closest finishes in years. Then, just seven laps from the end, Schumacher peeled off Coulthard's rear wing and into the pits for a second unscheduled stop. A miscalculation on fuel made the 4.4 second splash and dash pit stop necessary. It killed Schumacher's challenge but let Frentzen through for a clear run at the leader.

Right *Not a dry eye in the team.*
Congratulations from McLaren boss Ron Dennis (Allsport).

Catching the Scot was one thing, but getting past quite another. With two laps to go Frentzen, still pursuing, hit the brakes at the end of the start–finish straight. The carbon fibre disc brake which had already been glowing red hot, simply exploded. Frentzen spun out of the race.

Coulthard completed the lap, then began to cry.

For many people the most impressive fact was not that Coulthard had won the race – after Villeneuve went out it was his for the taking. But to win a Grand Prix after nearly 200 miles of flat-out driving, all but 15 miles of it with Michael Schumacher sitting one second back – that shows character.

Among the celebrations there was an expensive postscript however. The Scot had to pay £25,000 to a children's charity to honour a bet with Ron Dennis. There was also the question of having his hair dyed silver to meet another bet, with Mercedes team boss Norbert Haug who, in return, sportingly agreed to fund one of the biggest post race parties seen in recent times. Coulthard proved to be a man of character – and honour!

• CHAPTER ONE •

Scotland's Young Pretender

'I'M OBVIOUSLY NOT some hairy-arsed Highlander,' said David Coulthard, aged 23, occupation, Formula 1 racing driver. 'But I am immensely proud to be Scottish.'

With these words, shortly after finishing second in the 1994 Portuguese Grand Prix at Estoril driving for the Williams Renault team, David Coulthard both embraced his past and reached out to grasp what promised to be a glittering future. He was tacitly adopting the mantle of Young Pretender, the one who would attempt to follow two of the greatest Formula 1 drivers the world has ever known, hoping to take up where they left off.

Scotland has an impressive racing heritage. In the 47 years of modern Formula 1, Britain has sired no fewer than eight World Champions who have between them accounted for 12 World Championship titles. Two of the eight came from Scotland, Jim Clark and Jackie Stewart. They won five of the 12 world titles – Clark in 1963 and 1965, and Stewart in 1969, 1971 and 1973. This is a towering achievement from a country – and everyone in Scotland regards it as a country, no matter that it is ruled from London – with a population one-tenth that of England.

In a sport where every move of every car and driver, wherever it happens to be in the world, is timed to one thousandth of a second, statistics come thick and fast and, if you let them, can easily overwhelm the senses. But consider these. The two Scottish champions between them scored 52 Grand Prix wins, the six English champions just 85.

Including Coulthard's results up to the start of the 1997 season, the Scots scored 55 pole positions compared with 91 achieved by English drivers, and 48 fastest laps compared with 84.

Jim Clark's batting average, the number of wins compared with the number of Grand Prix starts, is still a record at over one in three – 25 victories from 72 starts. His 33 pole positions remained a record for more than two decades until beaten by Ayrton Senna, and the 25 Grand Prix wins were bested by Stewart, who scored his 27th GP win in 1973, five years after Clark's death. Stewart's record, in turn, stood for 14 years until Alain Prost finally beat it in 1987. Quite an example for ambitious young Coulthard to follow.

There is another element that makes the statistics all the more remarkable. Save for the 1986 season of Johnny Dumfries, driving for Lotus and playing second fiddle to a talent as huge as Ayrton Senna's, Scotland has been without a representative in Formula 1 for over two decades until David Coulthard took part in the 1994 Spanish Grand Prix.

Coulthard cannot remember when exactly he decided he wanted to become a Grand Prix driver, but his mother Joyce recalls his rigorous training regime which began at a fairly early age. Aware that the forces acting on a driver were becoming increasingly harsh, largely through the effects of aerodynamics, the teenage Coulthard used to watch television lying on his side wearing a crash helmet. Every 15 minutes or so he would turn over and lie on the other side – to build up his neck and shoulder muscles.

Son of a frustrated would-be Formula 1 driver, Coulthard was raised with a veneration for Scotland's motorsport heroes. Jim Clark was killed almost exactly three years before David Coulthard was born; and when Jackie Stewart retired, David was little more than a toddler. But the influence of both drivers has been undeniable. Although Stewart was to play a key role in his graduation towards Formula 1, it was Clark whom David idolised. When he finished fifth in Canada in only his second race he was immensely proud of the fact that his achievement had exactly matched that of Clark, who finished fifth in his own second F1 race, the 1960 Belgian Grand Prix.

Quite why such a tiny nation as Scotland has had such an impact at the highest level of motorsport has no easy answer. Perhaps Jackie Stewart was closest when he once talked of being driven by a deep-

Left *The Young Pretender, attempting to follow two of the greatest Formula 1 drivers the world has ever known . . . (The Scotsman)*

Overleaf *. . . driving one of the greatest cars in the sport.*

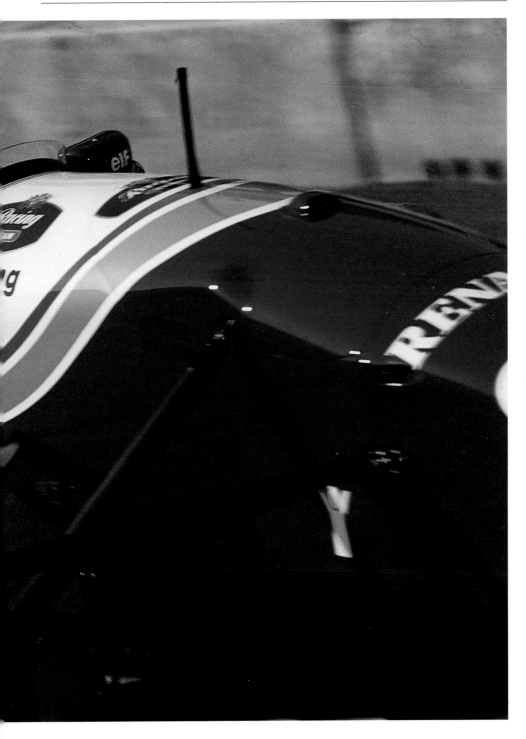

seated insecurity shared by both himself and Clark. Clark for example is remembered for his fingernails which were bitten down to the quick and, out of a racing car, for his complete inability to make up his mind or reach a decision.

There is a place for this apparent 'insecurity' however. Stewart says: 'If you are convinced mentally about your own superiority you are disregarding the most serious threat, namely the competitive element of your adversary. If you are so dogmatic as to believe in yourself to that extent, you clearly do not respect the level of the competition. I would far rather put my opposition up on a pedestal and be satisfied when I have shot at them successfully.

'It has no benefit at all for you to have a false impression of your own talent. You can kid a lot of people, but you can't kid yourself.

'People turn around to me and say, "Jackie, you've been successful". And that is true, up to a point. But am I as successful as I could have been? I'm really not sure. I think I could have done a lot better. Being successful is one thing, but reaching your true, ultimate potential, is entirely another.'

To some, perhaps those whose lives revolve round the hype and egotistical circus of Formula 1, his words may sound oddly self-doubting. To others – particularly Scots who, almost by tradition, have an innate loathing of the pompous and the arrogant – they mean no more than the simple expression of down-to-earth values and commonsense.

Robert Burns, probably the most famous Scot in history – as opposed to Jackie Stewart who is the most famous living Scotsman – was renowned for his earthy philosophy. It is a philosophy that David Coulthard also embraces: big enough to battle with motorsport's best, yet humble enough to do the washing up at the kitchen sink.

The former Williams test driver, promoted to race driver after Senna's death in May 1994, says: 'I remember turning up in Spain and absolutely crapping myself because I had not driven the FW16 which was this year's car. I had only tested at Jerez and Estoril. I was nervous about how I would perform. That is all I ever get nervous about.

'Of course I am aware of the dangers, all the usual things you hear about. I am a nervous person away from the circuit because I fear not being able to perform, not being able to be quick and not having the potential to win – that's what I fear.'

The Young Pretender meets the Old Master, driving the PSR Formula 3 car (The Scotsman).

Coulthard's father Duncan, whose personal involvement has been a feature throughout this success story, was never in any doubt that his son would perform. Indeed so convinced was he that David would become one of the F1 greats that he has retained every racing kart and racing car, every racing suit and crash helmet ever used by the lad including, it is believed, a 1994 Williams Renault FW16 replica prepared by the team for motor shows and exhibitions.

Whether David Coulthard would in fact live up to the performances of his illustrious countrymen, and prove his proud father right, remained to be seen. But the signs did look good.

CHAPTER TWO

A small village with big ambitions

TWYNHOLM, KIRKCUDBRIGHTSHIRE, population 280, is a typical Scottish hamlet – a handful of streets, a pub, a hotel and a couple of shops. Directly across the road from the village pub is a large, ugly shed-cum-garage which looks as if it had been reclaimed as World War 2 booty, transported to this unlikely site, and hand-built by locals looking to the future and all thinking furiously of the possibility one day, perhaps, of a job.

Tack-welded onto the front of this orange/red relic, in iron letters a metre high, are the words Hayton Coulthard. It is the trademark of one of Scotland's oldest road hauliers. The company was started here, around the turn of the century, by David Coulthard's great-grandfather and a partner called Hayton who was long ago bought out. It was continued by his grandfather, has been expanded by his father Duncan and will, no doubt, be tended by David's older brother, also Duncan.

The business thrives in a village so small that the inhabitants, according to typical Scottish wit, cannot even afford a village idiot, they have to take it in turns. It survives partly because of the intensive care of generations of Coulthards but also, one suspects, because – within a stone's throw of the Solway Firth – it is on the A75 Euroroute to the ferry port of Stranraer which is the UK's, and Europe's, gateway to Ireland. Duncan Coulthard senior is the man who supplies much of the economic wealth of this typical west Borders village set in a tiny valley between rolling hills. He is also a frustrated racing driver. He is, without doubt, the most frustrated racing driver in the history of Twynholm.

He makes no bones about this, and it is easy to understand why.

Innes Ireland, the first Scot ever to win a Grand Prix when he gave Team Lotus its maiden F1 victory in the 1961 US Grand Prix, was the son of the Coulthards' local vet. Jim Clark, another Borders man – though from the eastern end of the border separating Scotland from England – was the dominant force in Formula 1 when Duncan was at the age when he most wanted to be a Formula 1 driver but had, instead, to look after the haulage company. This was at the height of the swinging sixties when a whole generation believed that, one day soon, they could change the whole world. And while the Beatles sang *All you need is love*, and the Coulthards struggled with the business and planned their family, Jackie Stewart picked up the mantle of his countryman Clark and won three World Championships.

Duncan briefly dallied with kart racing locally. But the demands of the business, which was not in the best of health when he inherited it, met his future wife Joyce at a dance in a local village hall, and began to raise a family, meant that he could never realise his ultimate dream, to drive in a Formula 1 race.

By the time that Duncan junior, David and his sister Linsey had begun to grow up, however, the company was on a sound financial footing and Duncan and Joyce could enjoy their children, counsel them and, maybe, to guide them a little. And, Duncan may have reasoned, if one of them wants to become a racing driver, then who am I to stand in the way? More important, perhaps crucial in a sport that costs a king's ransom just to begin to compete, the Coulthards could, by now, afford it.

Duncan Coulthard would be mortally offended if anyone described the family as rich. But they are, undeniably, prosperous. Comfortably enough off, for instance, to be able to afford 'his and hers' Mercedes-Benz cars, a big house with a swimming pool, a paddock for the kids to play in. Comfortable enough to afford a small twin-engine plane in which Duncan is flown all over the UK visiting the blue chip clients with whom he does business. Duncan, 52, is a typical self-made Scot. A man unashamedly proud of the fact that while now mixing with captains of industry, he can still get his hands dirty fixing a diesel engine or have a drink in the pub with the lads. After receiving David's telephone call about getting the Williams drive in the 1994 Spanish Grand Prix, he rushed down to the pub to tell everyone. And you can be sure that since that great day Twynholm folk have become

This picture graced the cover of the February 1994 programme at Summerlee (The West of Scotland Kart Club).

F1 experts, following their young neighbour's career with personal pride.

Duncan likes to think of himself as a boss who can be hard and uncompromising at work yet as couthy (a Scots word meaning, loosely, down-to-earth) as they come in the rest of his life. Compared with her big, rough, tough and capable husband, Joyce looks to the casual observer like a mere slip of a Scottish lass – petite, slender, almost frail. Yet to describe Joyce Coulthard as frail would be about as accurate as to describe her son's performance on the race track as brisk. Joyce is a fiercely proud mum who would go to any lengths to defend her children. At the same time, she would go even further to ensure that they not only enjoyed life to the full but, perhaps more important, made the best of themselves while doing so.

While Duncan senior flits around the country maintaining eye contact with customers as he nurtures the family firm, Joyce keeps open house and provides, in the Scottish tradition, a warm welcome for all the friends that the Coulthard children bring home. David Cawthorne – now working at Lloyds insuring athletes and celebrities – was a school friend of David Coulthard, and shared a home with him in Chiswick and, before that, Milton Keynes. He still regards the Coulthard household as a second home. 'What?' he exclaims when you say you have been anywhere near Twynholm. 'You mean you didn't go in to see Joyce?' To him, that is unthinkable.

For Duncan, only too happy to let his children enjoy all the things he never had the time – or perhaps money – for as a youngster, it was relatively easy to give them their head. David Coulthard's first taste of the speed and power of the internal combustion engine came in the family paddock where he and his big brother played with motorcycles their father had thoughtfully provided. Just on the offchance, you understand.

To Joyce those early years must have been sheer hell. It was she who had to pick up the pieces when, as adventurous children always will, the boys came home with bruises, cuts, scratches and even the occasional broken or dislocated limb. She still recalls the pair of them side by side in the lounge with their arms in plaster, each one in a deck chair because that was the most comfortable seating. Her reward – one of her rewards – came on the day when David made his Formula 1 debut in the Williams Renault at the 1994 Spanish Grand Prix. Duncan was so proud that he could barely speak. Joyce was so proud she could barely restrain herself. Overhearing two bystanders pondering the identity of the new Williams Renault driver from the viewpoint of the opulent Paddock Club suite high above the pits, she was not backwards about going forward. 'You know who that is,' she said. 'That's my David, my boy!'

Given the Coulthards' financial circumstances provided by Duncan's labours, and the strong family bonds forged by Joyce, it is virtually impossible to think of two more perfect parents for a budding Formula 1 driver. They have always been supportive, of the sport as well as their offspring. When local kart racing fans – tired of travelling at least 60 miles to the nearest circuit at Larkhall – raised the money for their own track near his home, Duncan was ready and willing to enter the spirit of things, albeit at once removed, by sponsoring a local driver, Brian Smith. For Duncan, a shade too old to race, it was a way of keeping in touch with the scene and enjoying the vicarious thrill of nearly competing.

When David turned 12 years old the Coulthard family, especially Duncan, was rather delighted when he decided that he might like to try kart racing. Smith – who achieved some kind of racing immortality by first painting the distinctive Saltire pattern on DC's helmet – prepared Coulthard's karts for many of his early races. He recalls that it was an empty crisp packet and a fist-size stone which helped teach young David the braking techniques which he still uses to this day.

'It was his first time at Larkhall, and he just could not get his braking point for the right-hand corner at the end of the straight. He would either brake too early and make a mess of the corner, or brake too late and spin off. In the end I got an old crisp packet, laid it on the outside of the track at the braking point, and put a stone on it to hold it down. David showed complete faith and braked at the crisp packet and that was the problem solved.'

Smith remembers Allan McNish as the star of Scottish kart racing at that time. But Coulthard's ability soon became apparent. 'I used to watch David racing in the wet, and the control was unbelievable.'

Even in those days he was fastidious about maintaining his kart and keeping it clean. 'He used to spend hours cleaning and polishing it. Everything had to be just so, though he did not really know much about the mechanical side of things. That came later when he met the Leslie family in Formula Ford. Indeed it was amazing what the Leslies taught him in a very short time. He was very dedicated. We all shared this old caravanette, and after a Saturday spent testing we all wanted to sit up and have a few beers, but David used to keep on at us to have an early night so we would be up fresh next morning!'

The racing accident which gave Brian Smith the spare time to paint Coulthard's helmet – something to do while in hospital with a spine injury – also ended his own racing career. But the nerves which every driver experiences did not go away when he watched his young protege racing. 'I thought the greatest day of my life was when I won the Scottish championship. But when David won his first national title it was even worse. I was a nervous wreck and kept wondering if I had aligned the chain properly or bolted the engine on right. In fact I still have the engraved piston from the engine that David used to win, as a memento.'

This is how it all began. DC with father Duncan at his first race (Bob Geddes, Galloway News).

Fast forward now to Sunday, 5 February 1995 and it is a driech day at Summerlee race track, Scotland's premier kart racing venue near Larkhall on the outskirts of Glasgow. (Driech is a peculiarly Scottish word which means, variously, cold, wet, windy – but above all, depressing. Some say the word sums up the Scottish climate. Meteorologists can provide much evidence to the contrary, but driech is the way everyone remembers it.) Once little more than a distorted kidney-shape track less than a quarter of a mile in length, Summerlee is now a world class kart circuit built, and funded, largely by enthusiastic members of the West of Scotland Kart Club. In the often bizarre but always close-knit ways of the Scottish karting fraternity its reconstruction was personally underwritten by a local judge and enthusiastic kart racer. This gentleman wore a genuine pith helmet in the pits.

Just under half a mile long, Summerlee offers a choice of two circuits. There is a relatively fast open track for the extremely rapid karts fitted with gearboxes, and an equally long, but more intricate circuit for the vast majority who use class one, non-gearbox karts. Non-gearbox karts dominate the paddock. Fathers and sons – and occasionally daughters – huddle round the racing machines which sit on raised stands under umbrellas, tents, caravan awnings and, sometimes, the sky. Beside each kart is a car or van containing the rest of the family, the vehicles' engines all ticking over quietly, heaters turned to full blast to get rid of condensation and provide some welcome warmth.

The first race meeting of the new year is particularly driech but, for the fathers at least, relieved a little by the wee dram of whisky with which Scots welcome the New Year – sometimes well into February. In the paddock, perhaps a quarter of those who have turned up are there for the first time, the fathers prepared to spend what it takes; the youngsters, some barely eight years old, ready to do what is required.

Larkhall, or a track like it anywhere in the world, on a driech February day, is where motor racing all begins. Whether they admit it or not, every father and every competitor here at Summerlee shares but one dream, to make it to the very top, *to make it to Formula 1*. David Coulthard and his father always believed he would get to the top, even when things were difficult. 'We just knew.' Joyce's own personal philosophy will have eased any moments there may have been of self doubt. 'What is for you won't go by you,' she says.

At Summerlee they all know the odds. At the first race of the new season, it is 12 to one for the beginners. Great odds, perhaps, until you consider that only one kart driver makes it into Formula 1 every dozen years or so. Even odds of 144 to one do not sound too bad, considering the potential rewards, until you consider that the same scene is being enacted at hundreds of circuits around the world. But this year, for the first time in the history of the track, and the first time in the history of Scottish karting, the New Year race meeting is extra special. Because someone *has* finally made it into the bigtime.

It is almost exactly 12 years since David Coulthard turned up with his father on a driech day at Summerlee. Some of the children now getting ready to race were not even born when David Coulthard made his karting debut at the age of 12. But the links with the past are very real. Wander round the paddock and you will meet a number of karters who raced against him but, for various reasons, stayed racing karts. Karting is a branch of motorsport all of its own.

In a corner near the clubhouse a guy called Dave Boyce has set up a stall selling wheels, pistons, tyres and oil – the high tech consumables

Duncan Coulthard with Brian Smith, the karter who painted the now famous Saltire on DC's helmet (Wigtown Free Press).

Knockhill, November 1994. Six years after he drove his first race car at this circuit, David is negotiating with F1 giants Williams and McLaren (The Scotsman).

of the sport. Boyce remains one of David Coulthard's closest friends and the man who, even today, lends the Williams Renault driver a kart so that the two can work out for the hell of it on quiet days at Summerlee. If they are lucky, those in the paddock know they might even meet DC (as he is most commonly nicknamed), for the Scottish karters are a close-knit clan and this is where they often meet.

Over here is Derek Butcher. A former champion on two wheels and four, Butcher owns Knockhill in Fife, Scotland's only dedicated racing circuit, the place where DC first drove a racing car. Today, Derek Butcher is just another ambitious father. Over there is David Leslie junior, Honda works driver in the 1995 British Touring Car Championship (BTCC), veteran of Le Mans and the World Sportscar Championship with Ecurie Ecosse. Leslie probably won more kart races at the old Summerlee than anyone else. He once, though few people know it, out-qualified Ayrton Senna in Formula 3. It was Leslie and his father, also called David, who first put DC in a racing car.

John Cleland, former BTCC champion and leader of the 1995 Vauxhall works team, is today another ambitious father. So is Hugh McCaig, patron of Ecurie Ecosse, now BTCC challengers. But he is also a kart racing driver himself. And who's this wee guy who looks immensely fit? Allan McNish, once master of Larkhall, is currently development driver on the Lola Formula 1 project when he's not contesting the International Formula 3000 Championship in the Paul Stewart Racing team. Paul Stewart? Son of Jackie, of course.

The basic skills needed to race a kart successfully round Summerlee are no different in essence from those needed to kiss the barriers at Monaco in a Formula 1 car. The physical effort is, for sure, much greater in F1, the sheer physical effort needed to keep your head level under four G of acceleration, deceleration and cornering. Listen to DC himself. 'You're never fit enough in Formula 1. They are extremely violent animals to drive. They accelerate violently, they brake violently, they corner at amazing speeds.' But the basic skills, the honing of the desire to win, the discovery of the knowledge how to, are fundamentally the same. Karting is where you begin to learn them.

For those who have never raced, a few laps in a kart in close company with others gives the fundamental flavour of motor racing. Tuck your wheels into a bunch of young guys going for it and you can taste and smell the brake linings, the burning Castrol R from the exhaust – even, on occasion, dust and grit from the track. Perhaps the most lasting impression, however, is of the speed at which everything happens.

For those who persevere, there is an almost magical barrier to go through into a different time zone. For the onlooker, everything happens at amazing speed. For the novice, hanging on grimly for dear life, things seem to happen even faster. But for the seasoned campaigner, the mental and physical processes speed up so much that he has time and time to spare even when racing on the limit, his brain cramming maybe three minutes of thought into a one minute lap. He is thinking a corner – maybe even a lap – ahead, his body preparing to cope with situations not yet in sight. It is the first, and maybe the most important, step to becoming race fit. But karting is only one small step on the long road to being fit to race at the very top.

Nothing prepares you for the wheel banging, occasionally bone breaking, dash to the first corner

Coulthard's first kart race was on a track called Cults. This was much nearer to his home but, sadly, very short-lived. He remembers little about that first race 'except I definitely did not win.' But he did, far more importantly, survive it. For no matter how many laps you do in a kart, or a car, timing your performance against the cold reality told by the stopwatch, nothing, but nothing, prepares you for the wheel banging, occasionally bone breaking, dash into the first corner of the first race of your life. DC survived it, and came away hungry for more. Soon he began to pile up the wins, first in the heats and then in the finals at the end of the day when there is a trophy to take home and, if you are lucky, a note of your name in *Karting* magazine, the monthly bible of the sport.

When you are a junior karter in Scotland, or Brazil for that matter, the first title you have to win is your national championship. Not only does this normally win you the right to run a distinctive racing number – in the case of Scots, the distinctive letter S in place of a number – but it also gets you in the record book. Coulthard's first attempt at winning the Scottish Junior Championship took place in the autumn of 1982 at Rowrah, an English track so close to the border that it is regarded as more Scottish than English. When the Coulthard clan arrived there David already had a number of wins under his belt and, thanks to father Duncan, the best equipment and help that money could buy.

Given the aforementioned odds, what happened that weekend deserves a special place in the great book of motor racing history. For, lined up against DC was another teenager, Allan McNish, who would also make it into Formula 1 albeit, by the start of the 1997 season, only as a test driver. The year before Coulthard made his karting debut, McNish had swept the boards at virtually every meeting in the UK. Like Coulthard, and at an age when most children are still contemplating the change from three to two wheel pedal power, McNish had received a motorbike as a present from a father keen on motorsport. A typical cocky wee Scot, and a year older than the gangling, six foot tall Coulthard, McNish went on to dominate the UK for the next year. And as often as not, the results recorded 1 A. McNish, 2 D. Coulthard – then the rest. McNish remembers it well. 'Our fathers knew each other fairly well so we sort of hung around a lot. I remember David as being very fast, very smooth but, at that stage, not particularly aggressive.' (Later, after McNish had gone on to Formula Ford single seaters, and Coulthard ruled the karting roost, another driver destined for the top would play second fiddle to Coulthard's winning streak. Dario Franchitti, in 1997 driving in IndyCars for Carl Hogan Racing, would in turn take over the mantle from Coulthard.)

Tom McLaren, a former karting champion who now runs his own racing team as well as holding the karting concession at Knockhill circuit, was sponsor of the Scottish Championships at Golspie in 1985. 'I remember David as being technically very correct. He was fast and he was smooth. But it was McNish that showed the real flair. He had a style and a panache, while David always seemed to be chasing him. McNish was the driver that other drivers, those not racing in a particular event, would gather to watch at the first corner.' Coulthard's aggression, the real aggression that takes you through to the front of a Formula 1 pack, would come much later. But the boy was determined. And like his father he believed that if you were going to do something, you did it well. You never dropped below your own standards.

The following year, at Rowrah, Coulthard was hoping to consolidate his first round lead in the 1986 Superone series – then effectively

Leading the pack. DC in the PSR Vauxhall Lotus, getting used to the opposition swarming all over his rear wing (The Scotsman).

karting's Formula 1. The rain was pouring down and the track was awash. The previous night had been wetter than anyone remembered. On race day, a Sunday, conditions were so bad that by the time the Superone final came round the light was fading. Coulthard, starting from pole, was overtaken on the first corner. He fought back, in awful conditions when all he could see was a wall of spray in front but, after trying too hard, lost it and spun the kart to a halt. The engine died because a class one racing kart has no clutch, simply a direct chain drive from a sprocket on the engine to another sprocket on the rear axle.

To start a stalled kart single-handed, you place one hand, usually the right, on the top of the steering wheel, lift the rear of the kart (the kart weighs around 150 lbs) with the left hand, then run for 10 yards or so while crouched over and carrying the rear. Finally, when you have picked up enough speed you drop the rear end of the kart and, in one fluid motion, jump into the driver's seat and operate the throttle hoping to start a high revving engine from impossibly low revs. For a fit adult, on an empty track on a dry day, restarting on your own is something to be specially proud of. Coulthard, a 15-year-old on a crowded track in the pouring rain, restarted his kart and set off to catch the pack, now half a lap ahead. *He won the race – on the last lap, within sight of the flag.*

Did Duncan, or more likely Joyce, teach him a lesson once? You never, ever give up.

Following his defeat at the hands of McNish in the 1982 Championships, David Coulthard was Scottish Junior Kart Champion in 1983, 1984 and 1985. In 1986 and 1987 he was Scottish Open Champion and British Superone Champion. In 1988 he was Scottish Open Champion for the third season in a row. But by the time the Scottish winter set in at the end of 1988, bigger things were beckoning.

The next step on the path towards Formula 1 was about to be taken.

• CHAPTER THREE •

Cold as hell
but fast as fury

KNOCKHILL RACE CIRCUIT in Fife is Scotland's only dedicated racing circuit. Set in the hills overlooking the world famous Forth bridges, the track is just over a mile long and, if it resembles any other track in the world, it is Brands Hatch. This is partly because it twists and curves over the natural contours of the land, partly because spectators can see most of the track from any one vantage point. Circuit owner Derek Butcher – a champion motorcycle racer turned successful single seater and now a saloon car racer – has built the circuit from a once-a-month operation into a thriving motorsport and corporate entertainment complex open for much of the year.

The only drawback to Knockhill, apart from its remoteness for most UK racing drivers, is that it can be one of the coldest, most miserable places in Scotland. There is no racing over the winter months, therefore. But corporate entertaining continues, with companies bringing their clients to try a variety of activities such as karting, buggy racing, or driving a rally car. All this takes place alongside a continuous programme of improvements and refurbishments to the track and facilities.

Derek Butcher is a successful businessman. But he is also an enthusiast, and when occasionally he receives a call in the middle of winter asking if, perhaps, a new young driver can use the track to try out a car away from prying eyes, he can only give one answer. David Coulthard, after four years as a karting champion, arrived at Knockhill in November 1988 to drive a single seater racing car for the first time in his life. It was crucial to see whether he could make the jump from karts to racing cars. Not every successful karter can.

With him were two men called David Leslie. David Leslie senior is one of the gentlemen of motorsport who lavished upon his son David the same sort of attention Duncan Coulthard was lavishing on his own boy, but with a far smaller budget and a lot more technical expertise. The Leslie family had recently started their own racing team to run promising drivers in the junior formulae. Allan McNish was their first client, and he had swept the boards first in Formula Ford, then in Formula Vauxhall Lotus. Two years later, David Coulthard was their second client, his father reputedly having paid them a five-figure sum to fund the season.

But before that, a word about David Leslie junior who in 1995 is racing the works Honda Accord in the British Touring Car Championship. A former multiple kart champion, Leslie was born in Dumfries but lived most of his life in Carlisle which is just over the border from Scotland and, depending on which side won which particular battle over the past thousand years or so, spent much of its history as part of Scotland. Despite history and current geography, David Leslie considers himself a true Scot, wears the kilt with pride, and doesn't give a damn who wants to argue.

After a successful career in karting Leslie junior moved into single-seaters then, when he did not get the breaks into Formula 1, went sportscar racing with his national team, Ecurie Ecosse, and took them to victory in the 1986 World Championship for Class Two sportscars. And if anyone for one moment thinks that Leslie in particular, and sportscar drivers in general are not real racers, ponder this. In the 1983 British Formula 3 Championship which was won by Ayrton Senna from Martin Brundle after what was to go down in history as one of the classic seasons in that formula, David Leslie was the only other driver to take a pole position. He did this at Silverstone, then the fastest circuit in the world, and did it in a car that was desperately underfunded, woefully underdeveloped and, therefore, ostensibly uncompetitive.

Leslie junior was positive about David Coulthard's first attempt in a single-seater. 'We had ordered a new Van Diemen RF 89 but that was not to be ready until just before the start of the season so we borrowed an old Van Diemen and took David to Knockhill with that. The circuit had left the cones up from the racing driver's school and it was easy to show him the lines through the corners when I took him round the

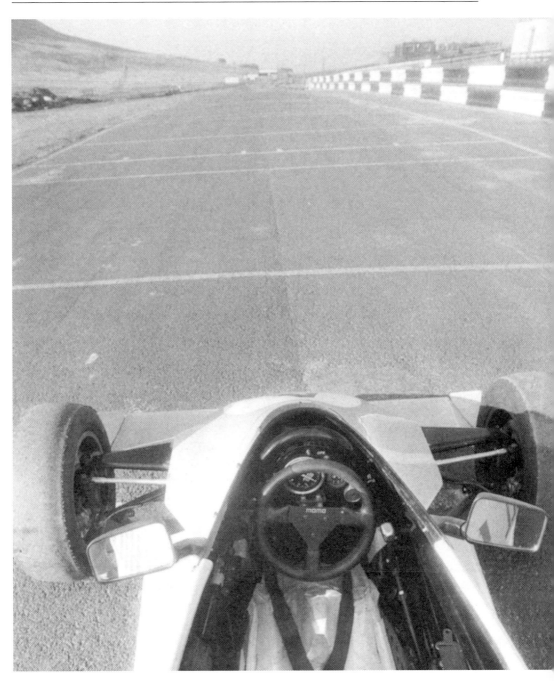

Knockhill Race Circuit in Fife, where Coulthard first made the jump from karts to single-seater racing cars (The Scotsman).

circuit in my road car. It was relatively simple, you simply kept aiming for the next cone.

'We set the rev limiter at 5000 rpm, then lifted it by 500 rpm at a time as soon as his times had become consistent until, finally, by the end of the day we allowed him some fun by letting him use the full 7500 rpm and finding out what the car could really do. He was smooth, consistent and did not fall off. With McNish we had allowed him full revs from the start with the result that he fell off and ended up in the mud. Our mistake.

'Duncan made sure David did it right from the start. He got him into the car well before the season and we tested, tested, tested. Duncan had given us a respectable budget, nothing like what some of the teams were spending but what we considered we needed to win. We tested like mad throughout the winter on every circuit we could find. We used the old, borrowed car at first until the new one arrived, then, by the beginning of the 1989 season, we had tested at just about every circuit we would be racing at.

'One thing that struck me about David that winter, he was able to learn new circuits very quickly indeed. That ability stood out. We knew we were going to be quick when we arrived at the circuit for the first race of the season, but Kelvin Burt was there in the same class and he had been winning races the year before so he was definitely the man we had to beat. David beat him in the very first race. Suddenly everyone sat up and started to take notice.'

Coulthard made a deep and lasting personal impression on the Leslies. 'He used to come down to the workshop in the evenings and at weekends and he'd take the car apart and clean it and polish it, and we would have to put it all back together again when he went home. This is in contrast to some other guys we have run who turn up every weekend and put their bum in the seat and that is all we would see of them. It didn't make David into a race mechanic or anything. But by the time he left us he knew what a spring looked like and what it was for, knew what a shock absorber was and how it worked.'

Neither David Leslie is known for suffering fools gladly, never mind

Right Thruxton, March 1989. Used to winning in karts, Coulthard pulls on his fire resistant balaclava for the first time in a motor race and ponders the next stage in his career.

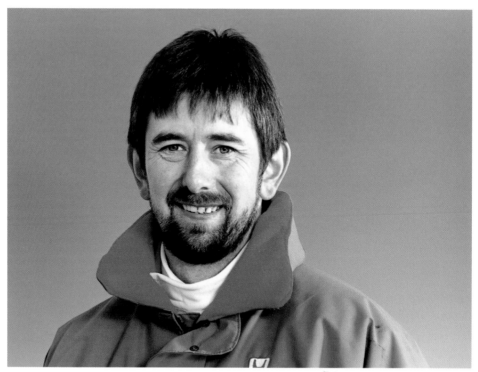

David Leslie junior. He described his new protege David Coulthard as Good, a rare compliment (The Scotsman).

prima donnas. Fortunately, they had no problem with the young Coulthard. 'David was extremely polite and pleasant. We have always had young racing drivers coming to stay with us all the time but David was the only one that ever stood up and volunteered to do the dishes. I mean, one guy turned up at the house and we brought him into the lounge and he picked up the remote control for the TV and started flicking through the channels. And we were all sitting watching the TV at the time.' Young David was also dedicated, missing out on the usual teenage pursuits to concentrate on racing.

Leslie junior knows how to race and, he has since proved, knows how to pick racing drivers. Not that he recognised Coulthard's potential immediately. 'I don't think David stood out as a great kart racer. He was driving a Zip in class one (non-gearbox) karts and Zip are best at making class four (gearbox) karts. I think the results that David had in his karting days were a reflection of his ability and owed nothing to the equipment.'

Coulthard was well prepared for the 1989 Formula Ford season. Before the first race – in March at Thruxton – David Leslie junior took the (for him) unprecedented step of writing to all the leading motorsport journalists telling them to watch out for the new Flying Scot whom Leslie described in typically understated terms, as 'Good'.

'How good?' we asked.

'GOOD,' said Leslie. From him this was thunder.

Coulthard, driving a bright red, Eternit-backed Van Diemen, won Thruxton in persistent drizzle. He got away third behind Graham Fennymore and Kelvin Burt. Fennymore, who had been on pole, was passed by both then, at the chicane on the first lap, Coulthard calmly outbraked Burt – and was never seen again. He won by 6.6 seconds.

Then he went on to win the next four races in a row – Brands Hatch, Thruxton, Donington, and Silverstone – on his way to dominating both the Dunlop/*Autosport* Star of Tomorrow and the P&O Ferries 1989 Formula Ford 1600 Junior Championships. And the winning continued, in what was the most competitive junior formula on earth because, as everyone knew, this was the first big step on the motorsport ladder.

Coulthard takes the lead on the way to winning his first car race after passing Fennymore (30) and coolly outbraking Burt (95), the man he thought would be his biggest rival.

The climb towards Formula 1 is full of the improbable.

The day before Coulthard's third Formula Ford race and third win, again at Thruxton, Nigel Mansell had scored one of the most improbable feats in the history of Formula 1. He won the Brazilian Grand Prix in a Ferrari that had hardly run more than a few laps reliably before the start of this first race of the 1989 season. Equally improbably, Coulthard was the man who would be chosen by the Williams Renault team to drive alongside Damon Hill in 1995 – in preference to Mansell, the 1992 F1 World Champion and 1993 Indycar Champion. But that was all still in the far, distant future.

Right now Coulthard was concentrating on climbing that motorsport ladder. At the third race, at Thruxton on Easter Monday, Coulthard, who had qualified on pole a full seven-tenths of a second ahead of his nearest challenger Kelvin Burt, went on to another win. *Motoring News* was already referring to him as 'the brilliant young Scotsman'. Then on to Brands Hatch where, although only second fastest in practice, he had become a teenage sensation in *Motoring News*. The paper described him as 'a star in the ascendant', enthusing that 'Coulthard blitzed the junior FF1600 ranks – this one is going all the way'. In the race he

In a class of his own – the bright red Eternit-backed Van Diemen was a familiar sight at the head of any FF1600 race in 1989.

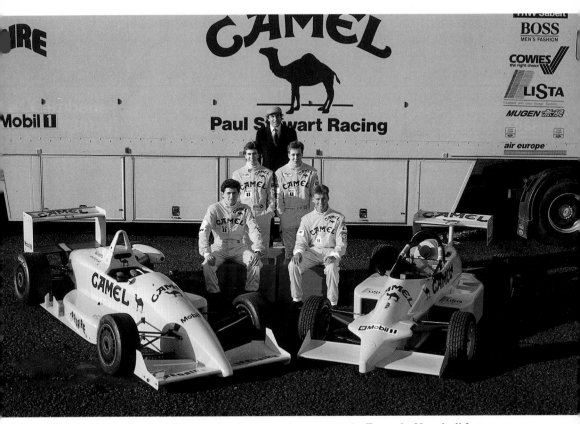

1990. DC joins the Paul Stewart Racing team to compete in Formula Vauxhall Lotus. He is pictured with (from left) Gil de Ferran, Paul Stewart, Jackie Stewart and Derek Higgins.

sliced past early leader Chris Goodwin on lap nine at Surtees, and that was it.

Occasionally, however, Coulthard could make an error such as at Cadwell Park on 3 September when, after taking pole from Kelvin Burt despite an electrical problem, Coulthard hesitated at the start, was overtaken on the line, then after seven laps of chase spun off into the catch fencing at the top of The Mountain. Cadwell Park? The Mountain? Once upon a time – a handful of years before, but half a lifetime to a teenager on a winning streak – another young charger who would make it into Formula 1 came to grief at the top of that very same Mountain. His name was Ayrton Senna.

At the end of the 1989 season, with both Junior Championships firmly in the bag, the Leslies entered Coulthard in the Formula Ford

Festival at Brands Hatch. Then the biggest international event of its kind, the Festival drew the cream of young motorsport hopefuls from all over the world. 'David finished third behind the works cars,' recalls Leslie junior. 'It was a very wet race and the works teams had adjustable shock absorbers fitted. We didn't. I know that if we had had the same equipment David would have done better, finished in the top two.' A note for the history books. In the 1985 Festival a certain Damon Hill finished third to a certain Johnny Herbert. Four years before that, a certain Ayrton Senna also won both Formula Ford titles, but missed the Festival when he decided to fly home to winter in his native Brazil.

A few days after the Festival Coulthard scored another win, only this time off the track. He was voted Young Driver of the Year by readers of the influential *Autosport* magazine in the first McLaren-*Autosport* joint awards ceremony. At the same event, McLaren boss Ron Dennis announced that Marlboro McLaren would back Allan McNish for the next three years. It was a gate on the road to Formula 1 for the first Scottish hope since Johnny Dumfries in 1986 and, before him, Jim Clark and Jackie Stewart.

The gate had also been opened for Coulthard. Part of his prize was a test drive in a West Surrey Racing Formula 3 car. But the best bit by as far as you can stretch your imagination when you are a young driver just barely onto the first rung of that awesome motorsport ladder, was the promise of a few laps in a McLaren Formula 1 car. He was to have very much closer dealings with McLaren at a later date, but that's another story.

To Coulthard, being named the first Young Driver of the Year under the new awards scheme came as a complete surprise. 'After I stood up I thought, "Did they really say my name?" As I walked to the stage they said that I was going to get an F3 test drive. I couldn't believe what they said. Then they said I get to drive a Formula 1 car.'

Afterwards, sitting with his family, Coulthard had a smile that was a mile wide. But it was not until later that the news really sank in. 'I went and asked Allan (McNish) what it's like, because he's tested one already. Now I can't wait!' But even in the elation of such a night, Coulthard retained his sense of proportion. 'I've got to keep my feet firmly on the ground. I'll just carry on with my racing and hope that I

Right *Coulthard leading the Formula Vauxhall Lotus race at Silverstone in 1990.*

can follow in Allan's footsteps. He's got a fantastic chance there and I am sure he will make the most of it. As for me, well, I've got something to dream about now.'

Coulthard realised his dream in November 1990 when he became only the third person after Prost and Senna to drive the McLaren Honda. It was around about the time that young Michael Schumacher, who had just won the German Formula 3 Championship, took the apparently strange decision to move towards Formula 1 via the Mercedes world sportscar team. Coulthard too would dally with sportscars on the road to Formula 1, and would win his class in the 1993 Le Mans 24-Hour Race for Jaguar. But that was still in the future.

For 1990 Coulthard joined the Camel-sponsored Paul Stewart Racing team in Formula Vauxhall Lotus. The Milton Keynes team, which would go on to become one of the most successful in the junior formula before moving into Formula 1 as Stewart Grand Prix, was chaired by Jackie Stewart, three times World Champion. He believed in a very hands-on management style.

It was the first direct link between the Scottish Formula 1 glory days and the ambitious Young Pretender.

• CHAPTER FOUR •

Young Pretender meets Old Master

FOR 1990, HIS second full season of motor racing, David Coulthard had joined Paul Stewart Racing. PSR was set up in 1988 primarily to look after the racing interests of Paul, elder son of John Young Stewart, otherwise known as Jackie. But the team quickly attracted a host of sponsors keen to be associated with, in the first instance, the Jackie Stewart name. Right from the start one of Jackie's aims was to use the team to set up what he called a staircase of talent to take young drivers all the way from entry level formula such as Vauxhall Lotus into, hopefully, Formula 1.

The team may have originally been regarded as something of a joke by the cynics or, even worse, as a rich man's indulgence of his son. But that would be forgetting what Jackie Stewart is all about when it comes to motorsport – perfection.

Formula Vauxhall Lotus, known as Formula GM Lotus in Europe, was a single-seater formula designed to take the place of Formula Ford as the first rung on the motor racing ladder. In 1988, when it was launched, the British series was won by Allan McNish, the Euro series by Mika Hakkinen. After that beginning, there was never any question that it was the formula to tackle if you were an ambitious driver.

Coulthard joined the yellow-liveried PSR Formula Vauxhall Lotus team at the beginning of 1990 and, thanks to his multiple triumphs in Formula Ford the year before, started the season as a runaway favourite. But if DC expected another walkover he was in for a disappointment. This was delivered in the first race at Donington on 25 March when he was beaten by Vincenzo Sospiri – though he did finish well ahead of his team-mate Gil de Ferran who came ninth. It was not until Silverstone, fourth race of the season, that he was back at the top of the rostrum. Taking second place on the grid, he snatched the lead at the start after Shinji Nakano (Christal Racing), on pole position, was unsighted by the sun.

Coulthard's Silverstone triumph was to be one of only two victories in the series that year. Even so he was just six points behind series leader Kurt Luby (K L Motorsport) when he went to Spa for a European series event – which was among the support races for the Belgian Grand Prix – to give him his first taste of racing abroad. With de Ferran concentrating on the European championship – he was lying a close second behind Draco Racing's Rubens Barrichello – Coulthard was happy with sixth place on the first lap when Swedish driver Kenny Brack tapped the back of the Scot's car and sent it into a spin. The rear of Coulthard's car just kissed the barrier but he came to rest on the grass, facing back up the track. Then, just as he selected first gear to move off again, Concept 3 driver Alain Plasch appeared over the hill,

Coulthard's Formula Vauxhall Lotus debut in 1990 was disappointing, following his triumphs in FF1600 a year earlier, but he could usually beat his team-mate Gil de Ferran.

spotted Coulthard, and spun. The back end of Plasch's car hit the front of Coulthard's in a horrific looking crash but, fortunately, both drivers were quickly out of their cars.

'I spoke to Alain after the crash and he remembered nothing about it,' Coulthard said. He himself limped back to the pits with a very sore leg indeed. It was only much later, when he attended his own doctor at home, who sent him to the local casualty department in Dumfries, that Coulthard discovered he had a broken leg. Paul Stewart remembers the Spa incident well. 'It was a really upsetting time for David and for his family. When they asked at first, the officials told them that he had been taken to hospital so they were naturally very worried as they thought it must be quite serious. Then they asked again and were told that he was back in the pits.'

With the next round at Donington just a few days away, and only three rounds of the championship still to go, Coulthard wanted desperately to race. 'If the decision was mine I would be back in the car at Donington,' he said a few days before the race. 'But I've got to see what the specialist says. I'm keeping my fingers crossed.'

He didn't race, and the 1990 championship was gone. Coulthard did however make the last race of the season, also at Donington, with no chance of the title but every hope of winning that race. He was aware even then that a driver is only as good as his last result. Coulthard made one of his fantastic starts from the second row and took the chequered flag at a gallop. Unfortunately, the marshals decreed that his start had been fantastic a fraction of a second too soon, so he was disqualified. By then, however, Coulthard was committed to a full 1991 season of Formula 3 with the same PSR team.

Recalling Coulthard's arrival at the team, Paul Stewart says, 'One thing I remember is that with David Leslie the year before he had been allowed to turn up at the workshops and handle the car. We didn't allow that and had to persuade him to leave the car alone and let the engineers and the mechanics work on with it.'

A word now, perhaps, about Paul Stewart.

Paul, a child of the original jet set, was brought up in Scotland and Switzerland, then educated in the United States. Like many sons of famous racing drivers of the sixties – Damon Hill, son of Graham; Jacques Villeneuve, son of Gilles; Michael Andretti, son of Mario – Paul wanted to go motor racing, just like his dad. Unlike certain sons

Left *In 1991 he helped establish Paul Stewart Racing as a major force in Formula 3.*

who were actively encouraged to take up the sport, however, Paul faced the wrath of his mother Helen if he even dared think about motor racing as a career. Equally formidable was the wrath of father, Jackie, who may be referred to (but only behind his back, and only in Scotland, and only by those who know him) as Wee Jake, but is nevertheless one of the most formidable personalities you could hope to meet. Especially when there's money involved.

If Jackie Stewart is your father and decides that you will get a proper education and put such fripperies as motor racing behind you, then that is what you do. At least until you have finished the proscribed education. Paul was effectively barred from motor racing until he was 22 years old. In motor racing terms – the terms dictated by people like Senna and Prost and, well just about everyone else in Formula 1 – he was effectively an old man before he had even begun.

Aged 21 Allan McNish, then the great Scottish hope, was already testing Marlboro McLarens for Ayrton Senna and Alain Prost. Two years earlier he had become the youngest ever winner in Formula 3000 and on the way posted the fastest lap ever recorded in the formula. At 22 David Coulthard was a freelance Williams Renault test driver and poised to take his place in Formula 1. But Paul Stewart was undaunted. Faced with such competition from his home country – he was born and brought up in Scotland until Jackie discovered the tax advantages of living in Switzerland – never mind the competition from the rest of the UK, Europe and the world, Paul decided to go racing at the age of 22.

As if that was not enough of a handicap for a budding Formula 1 driver, consider this. At the time Paul decided to enter motor racing his father, three times World Champion, was still, in terms of Grand Prix wins, the most successful Formula 1 driver in history.

Ponder the 22-year-old son of this famous father going out, alone in the car, and mixing it with younger, leaner, hungrier drivers with 10 or more years experience behind them. These guys do not take prisoners. Paul Stewart went out there and battled with them in Formula Ford, Formula 3 and Formula 3000. And he sometimes won. Courage and determination were qualities he had in plenty. Also, like his father, he demonstrated a shrewd knowledge of what the market required off the track too.

Left *Two young Scotsmen on the make. Paul Stewart is contesting Formula 3000 but he expects David to bring the team the prestigeous British Formula 3 title.*

Below *Team-mate Gil de Ferran had to become used to finishing second best, but the two remain firm friends.*

Above *Coulthard waits for the start of his first F3 race in 1991. The TV camera mounted behind his head would record some of the most dramatic film ever taken in the formula as he powered his way into the lead, often from far back on the grid.*

Right *When it mattered, such as in the 1991 Formula 3 Macau GP, he could turn in a front row qualifying position.*

PSR's aim was to create a rounded, all-in driver, a programme initiated by Jackie and nicknamed The Jackie Stewart Charm School. To this day Coulthard vehemently denies that his polished performances in front of sponsors and the media are a result of indoctrination. Paul explains the Charm School philosophy: 'The drivers go to learn how to speak in public and how, for instance, to talk to the radio in a different way to the way they talk to the TV. They really are different types of media and require to be handled differently if you are to do your best. We also tried to make sure our drivers knew how to present themselves. It is no accident that we have Boss (the designer clothing company) as one of our sponsors, because we believe you've got to get the whole package right. Just the smallest, unintentional detail wrong and it could mean that someone gets completely the wrong impression of you.'

In 1991 Coulthard would come tantalisingly close to bringing PSR the F3 championship the team so coveted, only to lose the title to Rubens Barrichello in the last race when the Scot had to retire after becoming involved in a shunt with Hideki Noda (Alan Docking Racing). But it was to prove a memorable year for the young Scot anyway. And one race in particular, the third round of the championship at Donington in April, was to play a crucial part in building his image. Not just what others thought of him, but how he actually perceived himself.

'David seemed to have this inability to put in a fast qualifying lap and often started from the third or fourth row of the grid,' Paul recalls. 'But then he'd make these fantastic starts and just drive past the people in front. Normally when someone starts from seventh or eighth in Formula 3 you think it will be a good day if they manage a podium finish. With David you knew he could probably win.'

At Donington Coulthard started from fourth and won the race on one glorious lap. It was one of the most memorable laps ever seen at the circuit – until, two years later, Ayrton Senna did almost exactly the same thing there in the F1 European Grand Prix.

Coulthard was fourth on the grid behind Rickard Rydell in the TOMs Toyota which had dominated the early part of the season, eventual title winner Rubens Barrichello, and Spanish Formula 1 hope

Right *Making the most of this by leading from the lights to the chequered flag.*

Jordi Gene driving a West Surrey Racing Ralt-Mugen. At the lights he was off, fast as a thief and – going into Redgate for the first time, that long horseshoe shaped corner which can catch out so many drivers – Coulthard had already dismissed Barrichello and Gene, and was sitting on the gearbox of Rydell. Between the chicane and Melbourne hairpin he simply drove past Rydell and was never seen again.

'That Donington race was the one when I realised that I could beat them all,' he recalled. 'I went for it at the start and even before I had crossed the finishing line for the start of the second lap I was saying to myself that I really could beat them all and it was so easy.'

Coulthard won the next round at Brands Hatch. At Silverstone in June, he had another blinder, starting from seventh on the grid but up to second place by Copse on the first lap, then he took the lead going into Becketts and was never seen again. In the eighth round, also at Donington, he seemed ready to do it all again. He was into the lead by the first corner despite starting from the second row of the grid, but then his gearbox jammed and sidelined him for the rest of the race. He took his fourth win of the season at Snetterton then, just to reinforce his mastery, nipped over to Zandvoort to win the Marlboro Masters of Formula 3 race. It was the fifth time he had beaten Barrichello fair and square, to the one time the young Brazilian had beaten him.

Back at Silverstone again, Coulthard made his debut on the front row of a Formula 3 grid. After fourth place at Donington in April, when he was involved in a clash on the first lap, and a mechanical failure at Donington in September, he went into the championship decider at Thruxton needing a win to get the title – providing Barrichello finished fourth or worse. The Brazilian started from pole, Coulthard from seventh which for him was perfect . . . until he tried overtaking Noda for second place and had part of his rear wing knocked off for his trouble, costing him the race.

Apart from his fantastic starts, and his almost Senna-like ability to go flat out from the green light, Coulthard also displayed the first signs of a truly adult racer.

Leading the non-championship event at Spa under great pressure from Jordi Gene, the Scot went into a sweeping left-hander going a little too fast. The car twitched under braking and started to run wide, opening up a gap through the inside for Gene who was sitting on his gearbox. Young drivers, especially ambitious young drivers in Formula

3, always go for the inside gap. But in the fraction of a second it took to realise he had left his braking too late Coulthard was busy working it out. 'I'd followed him (Gene) through there in practice and noted that he tended to take a wide line. When I made the mistake I realised it would feel really unnatural to him to go down the inside and I didn't try to defend the place, just concentrated on the exit line from the corner.'

'That whole season was a very important year for us,' Paul Stewart recalls. 'Up until then Dick (Bennetts, boss of West Surrey Racing) was the man to beat and we really wanted to beat him. We came so close. I think it was then that people started to talk about Paul Stewart Racing more seriously.'

Macau 1991, and the spoils of victory.

Anyone who hadn't taken David Coulthard seriously before was certainly doing so after this Formula 3 season – especially his by now legendary starts. Especially when he won his very first 'Grand Prix'.

The Formula 3 Macau Grand Prix is not of course a Grand Prix in the proper sense, any more than the Formula 3000 Pau Grand Prix earns a place on the calendar of the absolute top level of motorsport. But – fought out on the street circuit of one of the richest little pieces of real estate in the world – it was the perfect, high visibility race for the young up and coming driver on the make. Ayrton Senna won the race in 1983.

J.M. Barrie, Scottish born author of *Peter Pan*, is credited with the great line that 'there is no sight more impressive in the whole of the world than that of a Scotsman on the make.' Coulthard flew into Macau after the disappointment of losing the Formula 3 Championship and was very definitely on the make.

In the previous year's GP, the 37th, Michael Schumacher emerged victorious after an epic battle with Mika Hakkinen in a two-heat event which was as much a test of psychology as it was of speed. Perhaps realising the need to qualify well on a street circuit, Coulthard was second fastest behind Rickard Rydell. It took him one and a half laps to get past the Swede. Then he was gone, again. In the second heat, with

Coulthard rarely started on the front row of a Formula 3 grid but he often led into the first corner . . .

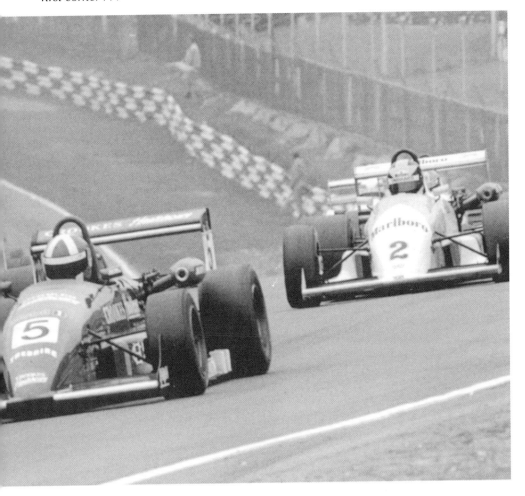

nearly 10 seconds in hand, he was mature enough to give way to Jordi Gene who lunged past him on the outside at Statue Corner, knowing he could comfortably shadow him all the way to the line.

For any ambitious young racing driver the Macau Grand Prix is a gold star for the all-important c.v. For Coulthard, struggling to put together his Formula 3000 budget for the following season, it meant some money in the bank.

It was in this 1991 Formula 3 season that Paul Stewart believes Coulthard really found his aggression. Strangely, Allan McNish believes this did not really manifest itself until later, in Formula 3000. 'Put it this way,' said Paul, 'you do not win Formula 3 races from the fourth row of the grid unless you are really aggressive.'

• CHAPTER FIVE •

Wheel to wheel with the boss

THE NEXT SEASON, 1992, David Coulthard joined Paul Stewart in Formula 3000 as his team-mate which, when you think about the importance drivers place on beating their team-mates, could have been a recipe for disaster. It is, after all, one thing beating your team-mate, quite another protocol beating a team-mate who is also your boss.

'We never really had any problems with it at all,' recalls Paul. 'I was very much the newcomer in motor racing, I was 22 years old when I had my first race, and I knew I had so much to learn from people like David and Gil (de Ferran) who had been racing since they were children.'

Paul's partnership with Coulthard in the PSR Formula 3000 effort was not, Paul now admits, all that successful as they had the right chassis but, until the F3000 Judd engine finally came good, the wrong engine. In such circumstances, when losing, or at least not winning, tempers can fray and occasionally snap. But the nearest these two came to a clash was at a pre-season test session at Jerez when Paul, on a slowing down lap, suddenly moved over at a place where, he now concedes, another driver might not expect him to. Coulthard, on a hot lap, nearly collected his team-mate and afterwards made his feelings perfectly clear.

'It was quite heated at the time,' says Paul. 'But I explained what I had been trying to do and why I'd done it, and that was really that. Looking back on it now, it's almost quite funny.'

Stewart's easy acceptance of the possibility that his team-mate might beat him was perhaps understandable considering that, providing they did not take each other off, he was in a no-lose situation. If he beat

Coulthard, so much to the good. But if Coulthard beat him it was the PSR team doing well. And while it is Paul's name above the door and he who has hands-on control of the day to day running of the team Jackie, as Chairman, remains the real power behind the Milton Keynes throne.

Someone, perhaps one of his sons, once encapsulated Jackie's approach to motor racing in a lovely piece of mimicry. It was delivered in a voice that was JYS to a tee. Arriving late at a circuit where his Formula 3000 drivers were taking part in untimed practice, Jackie dons the headset and microphone connecting him with the circulating cars just, as luck would have it, as one of the drivers comes on the radio seeking instructions.

'What will I do now?' the driver asks into the helmet-mounted microphone.

'Go faster, go faster,' commands 'JYS' abruptly, before demanding, after pausing a moment or two for thought, 'Who is this? Who is this?' It was not, for sure, David Coulthard.

Both Jackie and Paul had made no secret about their desire to take their team into Formula 1 but they were reluctant to do so without winning the Formula 3000 Championship, the one title which had so far eluded them. For 1995, in what is some sort of irony, they had hired Allan McNish to spearhead their efforts in the formula. The third Scot to sit in a PSR F3000 car was hired, in Jackie's own words, 'because the bottom line is winning races.'

Jackie Stewart remarked, long after Coulthard had left PSR: 'David was probably the best prepared young driver ever to enter Formula 1.'

Following his karting and Formula Ford triumphs, and his fighting performances in Vauxhall Lotus and Formula 3, David Coulthard's Formula 3000 debut at Silverstone in May 1992 was a disaster. He was stuck on the back of the grid alongside Hideki Noda while his team-mate Paul Stewart, in exactly the same car, was starting in sixth place. Even Allan McNish, on a virtually non-existent budget as Noda's team-mate in Team 3001, was two rows in front. But he too had his troubles.

'What had happened was that a thunderstorm had struck just after the qualifying session started. It was a farce,' recalls McNish. 'I had spun off at Brooklands and was just standing there watching the cars go

Right *'He's down to earth, straightforward, honest and, well, just likeable.'*

by when DC spun to a halt in front of me. It was ridiculous, there we were, the two Scots in the first race of the season, standing in the mud watching everyone else and feeling sorry for ourselves.'

In the race Coulthard finished seventh, just one place out of the points and, ever important, one place ahead of his team-mate Stewart.

After Silverstone, Coulthard retired at Pau, finished eighth in Barcelona, retired again at Hockenheim. This was particularly galling as the big budget PSR team was being regularly outgunned by the third Scot in the series, Allan McNish, whose drive for Mike Earl in the 3001 team was one of the thinnest shoestring operations ever mounted in the formula. The smallest Scot finished fifth in Barcelona and an excellent third at Hockenheim in the GP support race, but he was doomed to run out of money and miss the final two events of the season. He still, however, managed to finish eleventh in the championship, two places behind Coulthard but, for him, a glorious two places ahead of Paul Stewart.

After finishing seventh at the Nurburgring Coulthard and the Judd engine started to come good. He picked up fourth place in Spain, another seventh in Albacete, then two podium places in the last two events – third places at Nogaro and Magny Cours. This was enough to secure him ninth place in the championship and a reputation as the man to watch in 1993 even though, for the first season in his career, he had failed to win a race.

Unable to continue with the costly PSR operation for 1993, David and Duncan Coulthard fished around for the best deal they could manage with a reduced budget. They eventually settled on Pacific Racing then, as now, a team famed for occasionally achieving big results on less than big money.

Mark Gallagher, Pacific public relations and marketing man, has glowing memories of the young Scot. 'What stood out about David immediately was the great rapport that he built up, not only with the members of the team but with the other driver with us that year, Michael Bartels. You get drivers who simply turn up and drive, and they can convince themselves that it is them (the team) and us, or him (the other driver) and us.

'Suddenly along comes David and he's down to earth, straightforward, honest and, well, just likeable.

'I think he had a great advantage too in having a man like Duncan behind him because his father made sure that his feet always stayed firmly on the ground. The two of them were some combination. They appreciated that they had a tight budget, but they had a game plan and knew what they were out to achieve. They also appreciated – and not everyone does – that things can and do go wrong and that at some races nothing goes right on the day.

'If David had a fault it was that his qualifying positions never seemed to reflect his ability in the car. In a race he's one of the very best in the world.'

It was as if he was walking on water – he has to be the world's best overtaker

---

The first round of the 1993 season at Donington in May seemed to offer little hope of a better season however when Coulthard qualified a lowly 14th on the grid in his new Pacific Reynard, no less than 10 places behind his former team-mate Paul Stewart who was now partnered by Gil de Ferran. Coulthard, naturally, made one of his storming starts and was running as high as fifth overall when, on the final laps of the two-part race, his engine expired after losing all its oil pressure. It had, it transpired, been blowing oil all afternoon.

Then came Silverstone and suddenly Coulthard in the Pacific looked to be in with a chance – though, after qualifying ninth, he clearly had his work cut out, even with his reputation for lightning starts. Mark Gallagher recalls the race vividly. 'At the start he just went through them as though they were not there, passing on the left, the right, sometimes right through the middle. It was as if he was walking on water. He just has to be the world's best overtaker.'

Half way round the first lap he was up to fifth place right on the gearbox of Olivier Panis and with third place Paul Stewart firmly in his sights. On lap 15 Coulthard took third place by squeezing between the battling Panis and Bartels. Now he was on the gearbox of Stewart and stayed there for 10 full laps until his former team-mate made a mistake at Becketts, lost momentum coming out of the corner and dropped two places to Coulthard and the still hard-charging Panis.

'I have never seen Paul drive so aggressively,' Coulthard said later. 'Though I have to say he was totally fair.'

With de Ferran a comfortable 22 seconds ahead of the pack and cruising home, Coulthard could only realistically hope for second. He took it on lap 31 after second place Michael Bartels got snarled up behind a back marker. *Motoring News* noted 'Fastest Lap BY MILES, David Coulthard'.

The street circuit of Pau is, the drivers reckon, the biggest lottery in Formula 3000. It is also an intensely satisfying circuit to get right. For a Scot, there is also the historic significance of the fact that in 1966 Jim Clark won here and so, too, did Jackie Stewart in a 1968 Formula 2 race, effectively the same Pau Grand Prix.

Coulthard finished second again, this time to Pedro Lamy, and this time with Paul Stewart right behind him. Yet he so nearly blew it.

With four laps to go Coulthard realised he had no chance of catching Lamy and elected to drop the pace by a couple of seconds a lap to make sure he would finish. He was well aware of the possibility of losing concentration by driving at what to a racing driver is the equivalent of a quiet Sunday afternoon drive in the country.

Going into the hairpin he locked up and the car ploughed on towards the barrier. Even in the milli-seconds before the crash, Coulthard remembered advice from his race engineer. In such a situation, Coulthard had been warned, he should hit the tyre barrier as

Pau 1992. Victory eluded him despite a spirited effort. This battle is with Laurent Aiello.

straight as possible. He did, the steering wheel released itself and that was that. Or could have been. He found to his surprise that the engine was still running. Coolly replacing his steering wheel, Coulthard backed out of the tyres and into the race. He continued, more carefully, until the end.

Finally, in the fourth round, fought in the heat and the dust of the Enna circuit in Sicily, Coulthard rediscovered the winning secret. But

Who could have guessed what was round the corner – that in his first full F1 season, Coulthard would be leading the field at the 1995 Italian Grand Prix (Popperfoto/Reuter).

it came only after he had been barged out of the lead by Pedro Lamy who then, poetically, spun off 200 yards later before crashing out of the race on the last lap. Coulthard's Enna victory was to be the highlight of the 1993 season, however, as he retired at Hockenheim with a broken gearbox, and finished a lowly seventh at the Nurburgring.

Spa, the circuit where little more than a year later he would lead his first Grand Prix, brought his last podium result of the year when he finished in third place. But this, because he was forced to retire in the last two rounds at Magny Cours and Nogaro, was where he also finished in the championship. Olivier Panis, the champion, and runner-up Pedro Lamy were by then bound for Formula 1. Coulthard took some consolation from finishing just ahead of Gil de Ferran, but the future looked uncertain. He faced the winter of 1993/4 with no money and no prospect of a deal for the next season.

David Coulthard had some exotic memories however, particularly of his first ever race in the dark – in the 1993 Le Mans 24-Hour Race. At the invitation of fellow Scot Tom Walkinshaw, architect of the 1980s Jaguar triumphs at Le Mans and now owner of the TWR F1 team, Coulthard teamed up with John Nielsen and David Brabham to drive one of Jaguar's newly launched XJ220 sportscars in the GT class. Two other XJ220s were entered, one of them driven by Coulthard's former mentor, David Leslie junior.

The Coulthard trio overcame a catalogue of troubles which started with a pre-race scrutineering row and included the car catching fire, and later falling on David Brabham's foot when the jack collapsed at a routine tyre stop, causing him to miss the start of the race and take only a limited part in the driving. In the race, the car also lost an hour in the pits because of a fuel leak.

With only nine hours to go and four laps to make up, Coulthard sounded desperately downhearted as the team attempted the seemingly impossible. But they made it. It took exactly two hours, with the Coulthard/Brabham/Nielsen entourage carving 12 seconds a lap from the leader, Porsche. They retook the lead with three hours to go, and finished two laps in front. Despite finishing 15th place overall, the trio won the class for the Coventry marque. It was the new Jaguar's first race. 'I didn't appreciate quite how possible it was to recoup lost ground in racing like this,' said Coulthard afterwards.

Later, there was a nicely tangible benefit for an almost penniless

DC would not be one to lose touch with his old haunts when he became a world class driver (The Scotsman).

Scottish racing driver on the make. Ford, which owns Jaguar, and which had earlier loaned Coulthard a Ford Escort Cosworth in return for some public relations work, said that while he might be searching for a racing car next season, he need look no further for a high performance car to use on the road. That benefit was timely. At the end of the 1993 season Duncan Coulthard had an extremely difficult conversation with his younger son. He told him that the family could no longer afford to support his efforts in F3000: David would have to do so by himself.

The young Scot had not been idle however. He had by this time already negotiated a full-time testing contract with Williams Renault, following a season of testing for the team on a freelance basis. This would at least ensure that he could pay his way in the Milton Keynes house he shared with his then girlfriend, Canadian model Andrea

Murray, and his school friend David Cawthorne. But a testing contract – even with a top team – is a big gamble for an aspiring young driver.

It could lead to fame and fortune, as in the case of Damon Hill who filled the seat vacated when Nigel Mansell moved to Indycars at the end of 1992. Or, as Allan McNish found to his cost, it could turn out to be a blind alley. Three years testing and developing McLaren Hondas for Ayrton Senna and Alain Prost, followed by another season as a virtual full-time test driver for Benetton Ford and Michael Schumacher had left McNish at the start of 1995 with no real job prospects despite having clocked up an estimated 20,000 miles in the most competitive cars of their day.

During the winter of 1993/4 David Coulthard courted sponsors and talked to teams. He was competing with a score of other young hopefuls who, because they could not raise the £300,000 to £500,000 required for a full season with a top team such as PSR or DAMS, try to negotiate the best deal they can for the minimum budget. If you are good – as Coulthard knew he was, and as McNish knew he was in 1992 – you can sometimes persuade a team owner to take a risk.

By the start of April 1994 Coulthard, entirely under his own steam, had put together an estimated £150,000 budget. This was comprised of some sponsorship, some of his fairly modest earnings as a Williams test driver, many promises, but mainly debt.

Just two weeks before the first race of the 1994 Formula 3000 season at Silverstone, on 2 May, he had signed with Vortex to race their second Reynard Cosworth. There would be no time for testing, no time even for much more than a seat fitting before the first race. It was a desperate gamble. But Coulthard knew that to win anything, first you had to start.

• CHAPTER SIX •

The first
day in May

SEVEN LAPS INTO the 1994 San Marino Grand Prix at Imola, in a weekend already blighted by the death of Simtek driver Roland Ratzenberger following a crash on the Saturday, Ayrton Senna had the most publicly recorded death in history after his car came off the track at Tamburello corner and hit a wall. An estimated 500 million people around the world witnessed the crash, which was many times more public than the assassination, three decades earlier, of US President John F. Kennedy. Thanks to modern communications the awful news was known to people thousands of miles away before it reached some spectators at the Imola circuit.

Those of us at Silverstone that weekend for the first round of the Formula 3000 Championship heard the whole appalling scene described by the BBC's legendary Grand Prix commentator, Murray Walker. Anyone with a grasp of motor racing could see the crash was serious. (In the aftermath of F3000 qualifying, I was sitting in our new motorhome, idly chopping vegetables for the family lunch, and watching F1 on a ludicrously small screen when I saw the unbelievable happen.)

David Coulthard was at Silverstone driving for Vortex. I had left him a few moments before in high spirits because he had managed to qualify a virtually untested car on almost no budget in second place. For the young Scot – as the official test driver to the Williams Renault Formula 1 team – Senna's crash, and death later in hospital, had huge significance. The Brazilian, greatest driver of his generation, had been a colleague at Williams, and he had come to regard him also as a friend. Furthermore, as test driver, Coulthard was *de facto* reserve race driver.

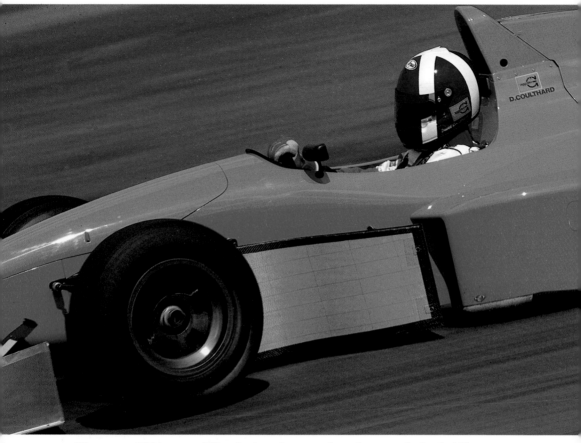

Silverstone 1994 seemed like the last chance saloon in an underfunded Vortex . . .

Though he did not know it at the time, (or if he guessed could never admit it publicly) the events at Imola were to thrust Coulthard onto the world stage and change his life for ever.

But for the moment, Coulthard remained focused on his present career. Just hours before Senna died Coulthard, up to his eyes in debt, had qualified a fraction of a second behind his old rival Jordi Gene and a fraction of a second ahead of his friend, but rival, Gil de Ferran. In his hands, as he watched the Senna tragedy unfold on television, was a fax from the Williams team wishing him luck in what might well be a make or break race. The fax was signed by Ayrton Senna.

In a plush motorhome just a few yards away from mine, Jackie Stewart was doing what he does best – or at least what he has done best since retiring in 1973 after winning his third World Championship.

Stewart was charming guests, many of whom had backed the PSR team.

Among the opposition that Coulthard would face in the next day's all-important race was Gil de Ferran in a Paul Stewart Racing car. Coulthard finished second, ahead of his old adversary. At the press conference after the race, still stunned by the news of Senna's death, he tried to dredge up some of his normal dry humour. 'I could do nothing about the guy in front but when I saw it was only Gil behind I was not too worried.' De Ferran, a Brazilian, was as devastated as Coulthard. But he too tried to find some humour. 'When I was lying third I said, ah, no problem, it is only David . . .'

As it turned out, this would be the last time the two great friends and rivals were to race against each other, for a while anyway. De Ferran, after losing the Formula 3000 Championship in the last round, went off to try his hand at Indycars. But before that, for young David Coulthard, motor racing's ultimate summons was about to fall on the doormat.

The Paddock Club, on the top floor of the main grandstand at the Circuit De Catelunya, near Barcelona, on the Thursday before the 1994 Spanish Grand Prix looked like something out of a guidebook extolling the glamour of Formula 1. It was here, among the carefully laid out tables, that Frank Williams announced what so many people had been suspecting for some time. David Coulthard was to be promoted to race driver. Coulthard – still gathering himself after a high speed crash a few days earlier at Jerez, shortly after Frank had arrived by private jet to oversee testing – may not have realised the full implications but it was a mighty gamble for the team owner.

Faced with finding a driver to replace Ayrton Senna, in a car identical to the one in which the Brazilian genius had died, Williams could have been forgiven for taking an easy way out and hiring a stop-gap driver such as the safe but capable Riccardo Patrese to steady the team until the end of the season. Or, backed by the team's share of the estimated £20 million insurance paid out on the death of Senna, he could have bought out the contract of a top driver and bribed him to join Williams.

If money had been a problem, which of course it wasn't, Frank Williams might instead have taken a flier on an unproven driver, cheap to hire. In the event he chose a middle course. Coulthard was offered drives on a race by race basis. And if Frank Williams was concerned

. . . but he finished second to Frank Lagorce (centre) after storming past Gil de Ferran on the grid.

about his decision he never let it show. 'I chose David,' he quipped to the assembled press, 'because he has an absolutely gorgeous girlfriend!' For the ambitious youngster – the first one to acknowledge the luck of being in the right place at the right time – this was the chance of a lifetime, albeit only possible because of a great driver's death. For the Williams team, Coulthard's optimism and blend of humility with confidence gave a ray of hope in a miserable season.

Outwardly, Coulthard seemed the cool, calm professional as he prepared to take his place in qualifying among the finest drivers in the world. As if driving the great Ayrton Senna's number two car on his Formula 1 debut was not enough pressure for a 23-year-old, external events added their own weight.

There was open war between Bernie Ecclestone, head of the Formula 1 Constructors Association, and Max Mosley, President of the sport's governing body, the FIA. On the surface this revolved around safety improvements rushed in after Senna's death: Ecclestone, representing the team owners, demanded more time to implement the changes, Mosley refused. At a different level it was seen by many as a power struggle for control of Formula 1.

The struggle was carried out, as are all such disputes in Formula 1, in huddled corners in the motorhomes lining the paddock, where multi-millionaires meet and gossip like housewives hanging out the washing behind a miners' terrace. The team owners, testing Mosley's resolve, held a boycott of the Friday morning warm-up. Only a handful of cars from the smaller teams went out. Not enough, crucially, for the 16 guaranteed starters needed before a Grand Prix could be run.

For Coulthard, already nervous that he might not perform, the boycott piled on the tension because it denied him the vital minutes and laps in a real Formula 1 car on a track he desperately needed to learn.

Between the half-hearted warm-up and the first practice session, negotiations began again in the motorhomes and a decision was reached. What it was, however, no-one quite knew. One team principal, only willing to speak off the record, drew a finger across his throat and announced, 'Mosley is out'. Max Mosley, the dapper Englishman in blazer and flannels, didn't seem to think so. He appeared in the press room overhanging the pits to explain his version of events. The explanation was of no real consequence then to the young Scot, except in one respect. Qualifying *would* start on schedule, the race *would* go ahead.

Coulthard was one of the first in the pit lane queue held by the red lights until the track was opened and qualifying could begin. 'In a way I felt calm once I got in the car and everything else stopped. You're in the car and no-one talks to you. I was in my own little world that I have got used to over the last 10 years or so.' Different pressures of course but it is still the same environment. You are in control.

Coulthard went out in the first qualifying session of his Formula 1 career and was 16th fastest due to a slipping clutch. Not perhaps remarkable in one of the two quickest cars at the circuit but, for a beginner, not bad. Crucially, he was in the race whatever happened now. Sixteenth fastest in the dry. Although the fastest times tend to be set in the final session on Saturday, the first session, especially if it is in

Overleaf *Barcelona, 1994. Making his Formula 1 debut in a Williams Renault, Coulthard ran as high as sixth before mechanical troubles disabled the car.*

Inset *What, me nervous? In a sport where tension is part of daily life, Coulthard has always been remarkable for his calm, commonsense and good manners.*

the dry, is vitally important because the final qualifying might be wet.

The pressure was now off Coulthard. Or was it? In qualifying, Andrea Montermini, on a hot lap, and absolutely committed as he came onto the finishing straight, lost control of his Simtek in that fraction of a second before everything would have been all right. Even seasoned drivers watched aghast as, seemingly in slow motion, the Simtek – travelling at around 150 mph – ploughed through the gravel track, exploded against a wall and, shedding parts every which way, spun across the track to stop at the pit wall where team members and press were gathered to watch the session. In the long drawn out anguish between heartbeats they scanned the wreck for signs of life, hoping for the best, but each fearing the very worst. *Another race, another death?*

Suddenly a lot of people asked the same question – who is this guy?

Damon Hill, under harrowing psychological pressure after losing his team-mate Ayrton Senna, looked stricken and, for a few moments, seemed to lose all self-control. The Italian driver was rushed to the Medical Centre and examined by the doctor in intimate detail. Afterwards he joked, 'the doctors examine my head, they say it is full of spaghetti.' I don't think anyone laughed.

In final qualifying Coulthard pushed just a little bit harder but never too hard, and qualified ninth. In a season dominated by Schumacher in a Benetton Ford, with Hill struggling to keep up, ninth was a good, solid achievement. You can win a race from ninth, but no-one does win their first race. In the history of Formula 1 only one rookie, Giancarlo Baghetti, ever has. He never won again.

Race morning brought another dimension. In the warm-up Coulthard was fourth quickest. Suddenly, almost in unison, a lot of people asked the same question – *who is this guy?* Coulthard knew. 'I was not overawed in the least. It felt so good. When I sat there in the untimed warm-up and was fourth fastest and saw my name up there with all these other names I thought, *that's me, I'm there. I'm in Formula 1.* I felt very relaxed with it.'

On the starting grid he was still ninth. For those of us watching who had known Coulthard for so many years, ninth was great, no problem.

'He'll take at least four on the first corner,' we told our colleagues in the press box who wondered who this new guy was. 'He always does that.' He took three, thrusting his car into sixth place on the opening lap, then settling down in a comfortable sixth place to watch the jostling between Jean Alesi in the Ferrari, Mika Hakkinen in the McLaren, and JJ Lehto in the second Benetton.

'I backed off a little while and surveyed the situation,' he would explain later. You get three guys battling for one place and there is always trouble, Coulthard knew from a dozen years of racing. 'Besides, I had never raced that many laps before (65) and wanted to just sit there and see what would happen.'

What happened was a succession of faults, caused by a failure in the electronic software which gradually disabled the Williams car. First the power steering went, then the throttle began to play up. Finally the gearbox started to go as well. At his first stop Coulthard lost a whole lap as the car repeatedly failed to get away. Eventually he got the reluctant Williams out of the pit and back into the fray. For a while it looked as though he was still on for an, albeit distant, finish in the points. In the Williams pit, however, they were taking absolutely no chances. Not just two races after Senna's death. Not with a 23-year-old in his first F1 race. Not any time. They pulled him in.

But he had done enough for now – perhaps more than enough. For once Frank Williams, who had originally put Coulthard in the car for just one race, made up his mind about something immediately. 'David did not get a chance to show what he can really do today,' said the team owner after Damon Hill had given the team its first victory of the season. 'He will get that chance in Canada.'

• CHAPTER SEVEN •

The difference between winning and losing

FRANK WILLIAMS GAVE Coulthard the chance in Canada, two weeks later, and the young Scot took it. He qualified fifth on the grid on a track he had never seen before, just one place behind his team-mate Damon Hill who, in turn, was behind the Ferraris of Gerhard Berger and Jean Alesi. Pole position went to Michael Schumacher, still on a roll that would effectively carry him to the 1994 World Championship at the very end of the season.

Montreal, one of the friendliest Formula 1 tracks in the world, is also, for the teams, one of the most cramped. The normally spacious paddock area is limited to a narrow strip of tarmac behind the pits and garages. There's room for a couple of caravans, a few tables to provide hospitality for the visitors and sustenance for the drivers – and that, apart from a single lane of tarmac, is that, before the paddock tumbles sharply into an artificial lake. Just how tight things are was demonstrated in 1994 by the sight of a courtesy van which plunged into the water just a few yards from the Williams enclosure after the driver made a mistake during a three-point turn.

Take the lack of space, add the near 100 degrees of heat, and Canada is a place where tempers can fray. Additional pressure was put on both the Williams drivers as the word was out that Nigel Mansell was coming back. Lured by the political skills of Bernie Ecclestone and funded by the effectively unlimited resources of Renault, the 1992 World Champion would reportedly return to the Williams team for four races which did not clash with his Indycar commitments. Though only *The Scotsman* ran the story on the Friday before the Canadian Grand Prix, the rumours were flying round the pits.

For Coulthard, with just one race and no finish behind him, there was the very real fear of losing out not only to Mansell but, if Frank Williams wished, maybe even to a succession of guest drivers to fill the Williams seat at the events Mansell could not manage. For Hill – thrust into the number one slot in those desperate days after Senna's death, but still openly, sometimes very publicly, underrated by a lot of people who should have known better – the fear was almost as bad. What if Frank Williams, in a radical move to rebuild the team, should elect to invest in the comparative youth of Coulthard combined with the proven championship winning ability of Mansell? We will probably have to wait a long time to hear Damon Hill's real thoughts on those dark days with Williams during the middle of 1994, but some of the pressures put on him went far beyond anything to do with gamesmanship, never mind sportsmanship.

Shortly after the start at Montreal there is a real old fashioned chicane which the cars, slowing from around 150 mph, have to negotiate with a flick right, flick left before the long, hard accelerating run to the right again. The Ferraris, their qualifying times confirmed, were coming good at last. Schumacher, surely, would be overwhelmed by Berger and Alesi first time into the complex. Coulthard, we knew, was always going to take Hill at the start. Always.

Somehow they all got through, Schumacher disappearing off into the lead, the Ferrari drivers managing not to take each other off. Then Coulthard, then Hill. By the first corner of just his second F1 race Coulthard was past his team-mate, perhaps the most crucial benchmark for any racing driver, and free to go hunting first for the Ferraris, then perhaps, just maybe, for the German in the Benetton.

During the first dozen or so laps of the Canadian Grand Prix Coulthard learned, or perhaps re-learned, one of the most important rules in racing. It is one thing to catch the car in front, quite another to get past it. Time after time he lined the Williams up for a run at Berger's Ferrari, but could not quite manage it. In his enthusiasm, perfectly understandable – what would you do if you were given the chance of a go at Gerhard Berger in only your second race? Damn right

Overleaf Coulthard was given a second chance in Canada . . .

Inset . . . and thrilled the crowd, finishing fifth, and winning his first World Championship points.

you would – he overheated his tyres and started to fall back, into the clutches of Hill. Hill, anxious to get past Coulthard and off in search of the Ferraris, was not amused as, time after time, his team-mate appeared to baulk him. Time after time Hill was on the radio to the pits, beseeching them to tell the Scot.

With the hindsight of a season Coulthard could have and should have waved his team-mate past as soon as it became obvious – and nothing is so obvious as a Williams Renault Formula 1 car right up your exhaust pipe – that Hill wanted, *needed*, to get through. Eventually, the team gave the order. Coulthard waved Hill through. 'Towards the end I was holding him (Hill) up,' admitted Coulthard. 'But to my mind I was not making it difficult for him to overtake. I was just leaving it to him to try and overtake. Of course, I am not one to move over for anyone until the team tells me.'

For the stricken team, Coulthard represented youthful vigour and hope

---

Eventually Hill got through and set off after the Ferraris. Afterwards there would be angry words, for now he had a race to run, a championship to chase. What Hill did not know, could not have known – and in the circumstances might not have been too worried about anyway – was that his young team-mate was in physical agony. His right leg had gone completely numb and, in places, he was having to push his right foot onto the pedals with his left. 'It was the most painful race of my life.' The problem – an old back injury causing cramp – would take him to Willi Dungl's famous Austrian physiotherapy clinic for a course of treatment.

Coulthard finished fifth in the Canadian Grand Prix scoring two vital World Championship points for the team in the Constructors' title. After the race Hill, still smarting, perhaps with cause, rounded on his young team-mate to journalists. Coulthard, equally angry, rounded on Hill for talking to journalists instead of tackling him direct.

In a team still stricken with mourning, Coulthard represented youthful vigour, determination, and hope. Frank Williams rewarded the Scot with a small Saltire emblem painted on the Williams race number 2 behind Coulthard's head rest. 'I had asked Frank jokingly before

Canada when I could get the flag painted on my car,' Coulthard admitted. 'He said he would consider it as soon as I scored some World Championship points.' When the Scot turned up for testing at Silverstone before the next race, in France, the Saltire was there.

Only Coulthard would not be racing in France. Mansell would.

Taking a leaf out of Hill's book from 18 months before when Hill, then a test driver, had hung around the Williams pit in Japan and Australia just to remind Frank that while Mansell was leaving he (Hill) was available to take the drive, Coulthard went to Magny Cours and, as test drivers do on such occasions, spent his days entertaining the sponsors, shaking hands and making friends. It was a PR triumph.

On the track Nigel Mansell faded away after the start, parked the Williams long before the end of the race (some suggest it was His Old Trouble, gearbox) and flew back home to the US. For him the race had been a disaster. Yet it had started so well, so full of promise. Mansell had dominated qualifying, throwing the Williams round the Magny Cours track to the delight of Renault, the French company supplying the Williams engines, here in the middle of France with all their important guests present. Damon Hill, perhaps sensing his career might be on the line, drew deep on who knows what final reserves of character – and beat Mansell for pole in the final minutes. He beat him by the merest fraction of a second, even on the scale Formula 1 cars are measured by, but he beat him, Nigel Mansell, his team-mate.

It was a glorious lap, fast and furious and, even from the fanatical Mansell fans, it drew a mighty cheer.

But at the start, the first time Williams had monopolised the front row for a full year, Michael Schumacher angled his Benetton Ford between the two in front and simply drove through the gap. Hill finished second, thus keeping his championship hopes alive. In the commentary box, sitting alongside Eurosport's John Watson, Coulthard could hardly believe his eyes when he saw Mansell park his car. 'Tut tut,' he told the listening millions, 'I'm afraid Nigel made a wee mistake.' Privately, his microphone switched off, he was punching the air. '*YESSS!*'

Such was the apparent ease with which Schumacher had got the jump on the two Williams drivers that the Formula 1 rumour mill began to grind out reasons why this might be possible. One of the technologies banned before the start of the 1994 season had been electronic traction control which regulated the power from the engine to minimise wheelspin and maximise acceleration. Was it possible that not absolutely *all* the teams had observed this ban? Might it also be possible, the more technically-minded pondered further, for those redundant parts of a car's electronic brain which had been outlawed by the new regulations to be programmed to, just for instance, allow three fast starts with traction control – start-up, rolling lap, and controlled start – before automatically erasing that part of the programme to avoid it showing up in post race scrutineering? Might such a thing be possible?

At the British Grand Prix at Silverstone, Hill and Schumacher filled the front row of the grid. Coulthard, denied vital time in the car for nearly a month, was seventh fastest, and this on a track where in previous years, in less powerful cars, he had been regarded as a master.

Fiery performance at the British Grand Prix, and another fifth place.

Though he would later moan at some length about how long he had been out of the car compared with Hill (drivers always, *always* want to beat their team-mate most of all, remember) Coulthard pulled out his own little surprise on the morning of race day. Even before the start.

He was fastest in the pre-race warm-up.

Between half an hour and 15 minutes before the race was due to start, each of the cars barked into life and set off round the circuit for the dummy grid. One minute before the official start they barked into life again and set off on another lap for the starting grid. Then, as the cars lined up ready for the start of the race and, remember, the third start of the day, Coulthard's hands came out of the car and waved furiously. The car had stalled; the engine had died.

The cars set off for another rolling lap ready for their fourth start of the session. Coulthard, having failed to move off in position but with his Williams now restarted, would begin his race from the back of the grid. At the start, Hill beat Schumacher into the first corner and won the race. At the back of the pack Coulthard was having a terrible race, but great fun. 'I spun on the first corner after passing a couple of people from the start, then set out to work my way through.'

By the end of the first lap he was up to 22nd out of 24 drivers, by the end of the second he was 18th, then 16th by the end of the third, 14th by the end of the fourth and 12th after just five laps. Immediately before his second pit stop, quite late on in the race, the young Scot who had started from the back was challenging Jean Alesi in the Ferrari for fourth. In fact he finished fifth, coming from the back of the grid. 'I'm a racer and I felt pretty good after that race,' he said, as if it needed saying.

Coulthard still vigorously denies that the stalled car had anything to do with any strategy to make Schumacher go round again for a vital, fourth start. 'No, definitely not. I pulled down on the paddle (one of two with which the drivers change gear) and the car just stalled. There was a hydraulic failure.' Coulthard's version is given added weight by the fact that his car stuck in gear towards the end of the race costing him his first possible F1 podium finish.

Next stop Hockenheim, Germany. AFR in mechanic speak: 'Another F . . . g Race'. But not if you are a Scotsman. Out on the back of the circuit, little more than half a mile from the start, there's a little stone cross surrounded by carefully tended flowers. It marks the exact spot where, on 7 April 1968, Jim Clark died when his Lotus spun off the track and into a tree in an insignificant Formula 2 race run in the pouring rain. Because of that tragedy, as big in its day as the death of Ayrton Senna, Hockenheim is no ordinary circuit.

In 1994 Hockenheim was to bring horror but, fortunately, no fatality. Millions of people all round the world watching the German Grand Prix on television witnessed near tragedy unfold. The Benetton Ford of Jos Verstappen was engulfed in a fireball during a mid-race refuelling stop. Somehow, mercifully, the young Dutch driver survived virtually unhurt, as did the mechanics who were in attendance at the time. But it was a close run thing. That blaze will be the abiding image of the German GP.

After the third crash the F1 wags christened him 'clout-hard'

In fact the whole race was dramatic. Hill received a pre-race death threat, Berger achieved an emotional victory in the Ferrari, and Schumacher didn't win the home race he so wanted above all others. Oh, and Coulthard set fastest lap.

'I had an indifferent time in qualifying but in the warm-up I got the car working really well. I was starting to understand the car and starting to use my own settings rather than Damon's and I got it going really well with the better fuel load on board.' (Technical note. Though drivers can and do share settings for the car governing suspension and aerodynamic preferences, the differences in their driving style mean that they have to develop their own optimum settings. The differences may be only marginal, but in the search for a mere thousandth of a second a lap, they can be crucial.)

Any hopes Coulthard might have had of a podium finish disappeared at the first corner where the young Finn first demonstrated the now famous 'Hakkinen chop'. 'Hakkinen bent my front wing in the shunt. I came in and had it fixed, then went out and set fastest lap by something like eight-tenths of a second or something. I was really flying.' Wasn't he just? He was not to finish, however. Gearbox again. But he did post fastest lap, covering the 4.2 mile circuit in one minute 46.211 seconds. This was a new record.

The young Scot was making a name for himself off the track too. Mark Gallagher, Pacific Racing's marketing and PR man, recalls the interest raised by the one-time Pacific driver. 'At Hockenheim we were entertaining a senior director of a major international fragrance company, hoping to get backing. He told me that he did not know much about F1, but that he had heard of a great new Scottish driver, he couldn't remember David's name properly, and if he could only meet him he would really impress his friends.

'So I went along to the Williams motorhome and told David there

Coulthard's fifth race, in Hungary, promised much after he had set the lap record last time out at Hockenheim.

was someone who would like to meet him. It was just before he was due to go out, and he was all suited up and carrying his helmet. But he came along to meet the man, and spent 15 minutes with him talking all about himself and about Formula 1. Three months later we had our new sponsor.

'How many drivers would do that just before they were due to go out – and for another team?'

In Hungary, again a new track for Coulthard, he qualified third behind Schumacher and Hill and, with 18 laps to go, looked comfortable for an easy, if distant third place. Then he put the car into the wall. Even as the car crashed, however, Coulthard was on the radio to the pits. 'I don't know what has happened,' he told his race engineer, every bit the cool-headed pro. 'I'm going to wait until the car stops moving and then I'll walk back to the pits and work out what happened.'

It was the third time he had crashed a Williams. The first time was at Jerez in front of Frank Williams on the day the team owner had jetted in to tell the young Scot he would be racing in Spain. The second time was later in testing at Paul Ricard, sometime home of the French Grand Prix.

Of course the wags, and there are no shortage of these in Formula 1, quickly christened him 'Clout-hard.'

The difference between winning and losing, as electronically measured in Grand Prix racing, currently stands at just 14 thousandths of a second as recorded after nearly two hours and 200 miles of racing, a record set when Ayrton Senna crossed the line ahead of Nigel Mansell in the 1986 Spanish Grand Prix.

But that is only a stopwatch, a piece of mechanical wizardry without the ability to think, or reason or make allowances for the multitude of factors which affect human performance. Ask a loser and he might well agree with the stopwatch, probably will. Ask a winner, however, and you will get a completely different answer. Winning is all about wanting to win, about wanting to win even more than the next guy, more than anyone else taking part. Winning is about confidence, about knowing that you *can* win and therefore will win.

David Coulthard had been used to winning from an age when most of us do not even realise the meaning of the word. Winning in Formula 1, the elite of the elite, is the ultimate competition. Could Coulthard win at the very highest level? Jackie Stewart has likened winning to finding a key: find the key, learn to use it and you can produce it as often as you want. David Coulthard rediscovered the key, or at least was able to pick it up, and get the feel of it for a time, in his sixth Grand Prix for the Williams team. The setting was Spa in Belgium, the track on which his countrymen Jim Clark and, particularly, Jackie Stewart had proved utterly dominant.

Spa is a long twisting circuit which winds up and down and in and out of the Ardennes hills, a track where the weather can be completely different within a couple of miles, less than a minute's drive apart. It is what drivers call a drivers' circuit. In the wet it is a circuit for heroes. Coulthard reports: 'I went there feeling a bit down because I had not had the results that I had hoped for but I was very, very quick in the wet.'

Coulthard could not escape the sense of history that permeated the Monza track

In the wet qualifying Jean Alesi, brave as a lion, took his Ferrari out and went half a second faster than anyone else. Coulthard, sitting watching the times in the Williams, thought, 'no-one can possibly go quicker than that.' Then the young Scot went out and cut half a second from the Ferrari driver's time.

Fortune sometimes favours the brave or, on a drying track, the lucky. Rubens Barrichello in the Sasol Jordan gambled on slick tyres for the last few laps at the end of the session and scored the first pole position of his career – at 22 the youngest driver ever to take pole – as the cars of the front-running teams fell into disarray. Coulthard, frustratedly waiting for the Williams mechanics to change his grooved wet tyres for smooth slicks, lost valuable time, rushed into the pit lane, then stalled in his haste and did not make a dry lap.

He started the race from seventh place on the grid but was into third place by the end of lap 3, then running a comfortable second behind Michael Schumacher on lap 12 – ahead of team-mate Damon Hill. When Schumacher called into the pits for tyres and fuel Coulthard, before his own pit stop, briefly led a Grand Prix for the first time in his F1 career. Yet he had not the faintest idea of what it felt like. 'I later found out but did not know it at the time because no-one in the team had told me.'

Whether he would have been allowed to win, supposing he had been able to overhaul and stay ahead of Schumacher after making his own stop, will never be known. On the run downhill past the pits to the legendary Eau Rouge, Patrick Head, Technical Director of Williams, noticed a definite wobble on the rear wing of Coulthard's car. Once again Coulthard was called into the pits on safety grounds. A long inspection revealed that the wing was indeed wobbly. But, after consultation, Head allowed the Scot back out. By then, of course, the leaders were long gone and he did well to finish in fifth place, equalling his best F1 result so far.

In the ragged, final few laps of a race which he had briefly led and from which he desperately wanted to salvage a podium finish, Coulthard pushed as hard as he could. At one point, when he went onto the brakes for the infamous Bus Stop chicane, he found a very long pedal indeed. Instead of slowing, the Williams rammed the rear of the Lotus driven by Mark Blundell. Blundell was approached by Coulthard in the pits immediately after the race. Coulthard apologised and explained what had happened. Blundell understood. Every racing driver knows what it means to push too hard, especially if the eyes of the world are upon you.

Events in Spa, however, were about to take a turn for the dramatic, a turn that would virtually guarantee Coulthard would not be allowed to win in his remaining races.

An FIA steward, examining the regulation wooden plank beneath Schumacher's car, ruled it illegal and the German was disqualified. The plank, a large sheet of plywood, 10mm deep, fitted to destroy any aerodynamic benefits from the shaped underneath of the cars, was one of a number of changes instituted by the FIA after Senna's death in an effort to slow the cars and make racing safer. A 10 per cent allowance for wear was built into the rules but any other deviation was regarded as a breach of the rules and the offending team, and driver, would be excluded from the results.

It seemed that Schumacher had lost Spa therefore. Coulthard moved up to fourth place overall but, far more significant, Damon Hill – 13.662 seconds behind Schumacher at the finish line – was now race

But after his first crash during a race he could only walk away.

'Nigel Mansell, in MY car, Frank? Och, come on . . !'

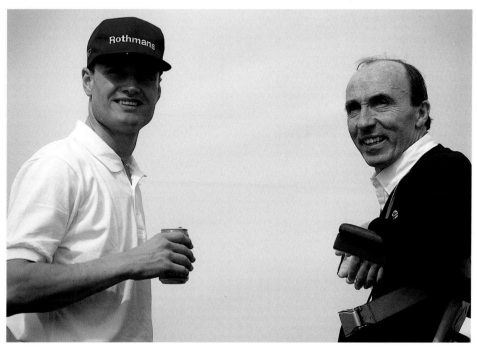

winner. The 1994 World Championship, so long seemingly a one-horse race, was suddenly back on.

A few days later the World Motor Sport Council in Paris confirmed Schumacher's two race ban for ignoring the black flag during the British Grand Prix at Silverstone. The black flag had been unfurled to call the German into the pits for a 10 second stop/go penalty imposed because he had overtaken pole position Hill and not kept to grid order on the warm-up lap before the race.

Schumacher, of all people, should have known that rule for it is instilled in drivers from their very first race. On the rolling warm-up lap, the pole position man controls the pace of the cars behind, and there can be no question at all about it. In karting, as in Formula 1, the pole position man may choose to get to his position on the front of the grid as fast as he possibly can. Or, if he has a mind to and he thinks it might work, he can wander round at a snail's pace hoping that his rivals behind may overheat their engine, overcool their tyres, or perhaps simply foul a plug.

It is, unofficially of course, just another good reason to try to start from pole. Screwing up this most basic rule cost Schumacher potential wins at the next two races – Italy, then Portugal. If, in his absence, Hill could win these races, they would not renew the battle until the penultimate race in Japan, and then only one point apart. Coulthard's role from now on would be a bit part. His job was to score points for Williams in the Constructors' Championship and, above all else, to help Hill win the world title.

Monza is a track which stirs the very soul of racing drivers. If any Grand Prix circuit can claim to be the home of motor racing it is Monza, one of the fastest tracks in the world where, in 1971, Peter Gethin won what is still the fastest Grand Prix in history at an *average* speed of 150.755 mph. That was in the days before safety chicanes killed such huge speeds. Gethin won from three others all nose to tail after nearly 200 miles of racing.

For a Scottish driver, however, it possibly means even more. It was at Monza in 1965 that Jackie Stewart scored his first Grand Prix victory. The runner-up? An English driver called Graham Hill. It was at Monza that Jim Clark – even though he eventually lost – produced what is still, more than a quarter of a century later, regarded as his greatest race, one of the milestone races in the history of the sport. Clark had lost his lead with a puncture and fell a full lap behind the leaders during his slow speed trip to the pits and while the tyre was changed. He then came back, caught the leaders, unlapped himself, caught them again and retook the lead – only to run out of fuel within sight of the flag.

David Coulthard could not escape the sense of history that permeated the Monza track when he arrived there in September 1994 for only the seventh race of his F1 career. It was a race that just *had* to be packed with drama. He did not disappoint, for it proved to be the second of three consecutive events where he could have won, after surviving the first corner pile-up which forced the restart.

In the race I felt very strong – I felt I could have gone faster than Damon

At Monza, Coulthard had what he considered his real breakthrough race because, finally, he went into the lead and, for the first time, knew it. 'I was looking very strong in qualifying because I was gaining in experience and confidence all the time. I was quicker than Damon in the first qualifying, then the engine blew up in the second session on my first flying lap so I ended up fifth on the grid.'

The record books – pole position, fastest lap, winner – tell some of the story of Formula 1, but they cannot hope to tell it all. Something akin to sibling rivalry comes into it too. Allan McNish sums it up beautifully. 'No matter what else is going on, your team-mate is the only one with exactly the same equipment as you, and to a driver that is all that matters, measuring yourself against someone in identical equipment and winning.'

Coulthard was faster than Damon in the first practice. In his mind, that was all that counted. He had *won*. 'In the race, my best race, I felt very strong, very comfortable, and I felt that I could have gone quicker than Damon. I led the race for a few laps, then they asked me to let Damon past.' If Damon was going to pass him, the Scot reasoned, then he could at least make it look interesting for the spectators. The team had other ideas. 'I knew that I would respond ultimately to whatever orders the team gave me and I was thinking about letting him past when he caught up. I could not have waited 35 seconds or something. I could not have made myself look foolish.'

But the team came on and said, 'let Damon past.'

'I said, no, he can pass when he is closer.

'They came back on the radio and said, let him past.

'I replied, not close enough, I'll let him by when he is closer.

'They came back on and said, look, MOVE OVER.

'So I moved over.

'But it was nice. I had had so many bad races with the car stuck in gear and times when I expected something to happen.'

Something did happen. The almost unbelieveable in a team like Williams happened. But he was not unhappy. 'That was my best race of the year. I was in control and well within myself. I thoroughly believed I could win that race.'

The unbelievable – 'I ran out of fuel.'

Watched by thousands at the track and millions on television, Coulthard unbuckled himself, climbed out of the car, then ran back to the pits. Might he, we wondered, be rushing back to discuss the finer details of weights and measures with the Williams fuel man? No, said Coulthard. 'I ran back to the pits because I saw the mood of the crowd, knew that Ferrari had not won and wanted to get the hell out of there before they invaded the track.'

Though Coulthard considered Monza his best race of the 1994 season so far and was happy to leave it at that, World Championship considerations of course meant that Coulthard had to let Damon Hill past. But something had changed, perhaps for ever, inside Coulthard's brain. Something not unrelated to confidence.

'You could argue that Damon was only racing against the third placed man in the race because he knew that I would have to let him past. So I am not foolish enough to think that he could not have gone quicker. *But I could have gone quicker too.*'

• CHAPTER EIGHT •

Sometimes coming second can be enough

COULTHARD ARRIVED AT the Estoril circuit near Lisbon knowing that he had to secure a podium finish in his last race of 1994 for Williams. The young Scot desperately wanted a result to help ensure that, when it came to choosing new drivers for 1995, the team managers would have him top of their shopping lists.

With Schumacher sitting out the second race ban and the self-evident fact that Damon Hill would have to be allowed to win the Portuguese Grand Prix to keep the championship alive, Coulthard knew that second place was all he could hope for. He knew what he had to do. Or did he? With Mansell scheduled to take his seat and no concrete word from Frank Williams for next season, might he simply just go for the win and to hell with it? Risk all on the big play?

In the Friday practice Hill almost made the decision for him when he wrecked his car during the second qualifying session after a spectacular roll – locking wheels with the spinning Eddie Irvine's Jordan Hart – trying to beat Berger's provisional pole position time. Hill, visibly shaken by the first occasion he had ever been upside down in a car, was, thankfully, unhurt.

Coulthard took provisional third place on the grid three-tenths of a second behind his team-mate and under a second behind Berger. The Friday line-up survived for the start of Sunday's race. Would Coulthard, we wondered, emerge first or second from the first corner and, if he emerged first, then what? At the start the Scot surged past Hill and nearly took Berger before settling down to watch on Berger's tail. While Hill relaxed and worked out the tactics of the race, Coulthard started to push the Ferrari driver. 'Gerhard was pushing it hard at the start. I watched his driving start to get ragged as his tyres went off. Then I started to think about pushing him into a mistake.'

In his eighth race, the 23-year-old Scot was thinking of manoeuvring race leader Gerhard Berger – one of the fastest and most experienced drivers on the track, in a Ferrari – into a mistake. On the eighth lap the Ferrari's transmission packed up and Berger parked his stricken car neatly at the side of the circuit. Coulthard was suddenly leading and with a clear track ahead of him. It was an experience to savour.

'I was pulling away and leading a Grand Prix and that felt fantastic. I was leading, I was genuinely leading and the car was performing and I was doing the job. I was pushing, but I did not feel able to push with the same disregard as you do, say, in Formula 3000. In F3000 you pay your money and you do your job. In Formula 1 it is a fine balance between showing how quick you are and getting the job done to win the points.'

On lap 11, pulling away from Hill who was now a distant second, he set fastest lap. On lap 12 he beat his own time with what was to remain fastest lap of the race. By the first pit stop he was six seconds clear of Hill and, though he lost a second in the pit stop, was still well clear when they had both rejoined the race.

Coulthard's lead was to last until the 28th lap when, under orders to let Hill through, Coulthard moved over in traffic. He then dutifully followed his leader to the chequered flag lapping everyone up to fifth place, and helping to give the Williams team its first one/two formation finish of the season.

After the traditional champagne spraying on the podium where the Scot said he was happier for the mechanics than he was for himself, he was able to voice his thoughts on his F1 career so far. 'I've never raced with Schumacher (racing means wheel to wheel combat rather than simply taking part in the same event) though it would have been extremely difficult to beat him because he is so confident. I think I was capable of winning during the last three races. You've got to prove to yourself first that you can win. At this level a lot of Schumacher's time comes from his confidence.'

The podium smile belied his feelings. 'I was not as happy as maybe my face showed. I was happier for my mechanics than I was for myself because I wanted to be in that number one spot. It just made me realise

*In action at Estoril
where he simply had
to get a result.*

*Estoril, and the line-up went Hill,
Coulthard, Hakkinen.
Williams achieved its
first one-two
formation finish of the
1994 season, and
Coulthard got the
podium result he
needed (ICN UK
Bureau).*

*'I think I was capable
of winning during the
last three races.'*

at that moment that it does not matter what formula you are racing in. When you want to win, you want to win.'

No matter how hard you want to win however, first you need to take part – and in Formula 1 you need a competitive car which, most years, means a Williams, a Ferrari, a McLaren or, latterly, a Benetton. As he left the Estoril circuit for the half hour drive to Lisbon airport after the greatest success of his career, Coulthard had none of those. He had nothing, in fact, except his original testing contract with Frank Williams who had let it be known that the document included an option on the Scot for 1995.

Worse, far worse, Nigel Mansell was about to take over *his* car for the last three races of the season which, because the battle for the title between Hill and Schumacher was boiling nicely to a climax, would attract even more media publicity. It didn't help to know that for this service Mansell was reportedly receiving around £1 million *per race*, whereas Coulthard was still on a relatively modest test driver's pay plus about £5,000 a race.

Mansell, aged 41, was an old, old man in a sport which favours the faster reactions of younger men, but he was one of the greats of the Senna/Prost era. He had won the Formula 1 and Indycar titles in successive seasons and, even his greatest detractors had to admit, he was one of the great all-time chargers. Not to say crowd-pullers. Nigel Mansell, in the car, was Hollywood's version of how a real racing driver should be. Smoking tyres, locked brakes, wild slides, and corny as they come. Oh, and those mad, breathtaking charges through from the back of the grid, often to win. Renault, having won a world title with Mansell before, accepting he was a known quantity and wanting maximum media coverage, wanted Mansell.

State-owned, but soon to be privatised, Renault needed more than a knowing wink from the French finance ministry to survive. It needed image, sales and profits. Perhaps, since the retirement of Prost and the death of Senna, Mansell was the only big name star. So much the better, thought Renault.

To Bernie Ecclestone, who charges each circuit a hefty fee to stage a Grand Prix, a fee based on attendance as much as any other earning

Right *A Formula 1 driver's responsibilities are many and varied . . . on the Piper B oil rig* (ICN UK Bureau).

power, Mansell is simply money in the bank. An astonishing 50,000 more spectators turned up to see Mansell winning the British Grand Prix in 1992 than paid to see Hill win the same event two years later. At up to £300 a head for the full, three-day event, this adds up to a tidy £15 million extra income – from just one event.

Coulthard elected to attend all the remaining races in the 1994 season. With someone as temperamental and, we must assume, as nervous as Mansell during his much hyped comeback, the presence of his younger rival in the pits, the paddock, the motorhome, might just rattle him enough. Coulthard duly turned up in the pits for the European Grand Prix in Jerez, where Mansell, we understand, was not in the least amused. The Young Pretender also maintained the pressure in both Japan and Australia.

But even before the start of the European race, things were to change dramatically and, as always in Formula 1, at great speed. Responding to one of three messages left on his telephone answering machine from top teams within a matter of hours of each other, Coulthard had dinner at Jerez with McLaren boss Ron Dennis. After seeking the advice of his management company, IMG, Coulthard signed a contract of intent with McLaren which, we had just learned, were to have Mercedes power, and money, for 1995.

Quite what the wily Dennis was up to is not yet officially recorded. Dennis is hardly the most forthcoming team owner. But the most popular theory was that he used the situation to test the strength of current contracts in Formula 1. Aside from a 'little' money in legal fees (a year or more's wages to most of us but simply loose change in Formula 1 terms) Dennis might or might not get Coulthard (whose dream car for the road, incidentally, was a Mercedes 500SL which naturally Mercedes-Benz would be only too happy to supply). But he would certainly get the measure of the strength of contracts. As a fringe benefit, of course, Dennis would also wind up his old rival Frank Williams. Rather nicely in fact.

And if Williams won, and McLaren lost the services of Coulthard on this occasion, well Dennis had probably caused the wages of the young Scot to be upped by a considerable amount and, well, there would always be another time and surely Coulthard would remember to whom he owed a favour. Coulthard too could only win by this manoeuvre. The move either forced Frank Williams into coming up with a full season's racing alongside Hill, who had already re-signed for 1995, or it freed him to join McLaren which, in a new season, with a new engine formula and all new design, might well turn out to be a winner again.

Young Coulthard knows his own worth, and is undoubtedly canny in business. Throughout his racing career he has also been widely liked for being courteous, straightforward, and approachable. His regard for the people who backed his career, particularly in the early stages, is almost legendary. He inspires unflagging loyalty from those who become involved with him, as witnessed by the number of names – Crookes Healthcare, Eternit, and Highland Spring to name but three – who have stuck with him. This anecdote gives an idea why.

Williams might choose the Old Lionheart or the Young Pretender – it was a finely balanced as that

On the eve of the storm over his contractual wrangle between Williams and McLaren, DC spent an evening at an indoor kart racing centre on the outskirts of Glasgow with Farrah Trousers and their guests – sales people from Ralph Slater Ltd, the company which, according to the Guinness Book of Records, boasts the biggest menswear department in the world. While DC, resplendent in his Williams racing suit and famous Saltire helmet, took part in a seemingly endless series of kart races, between times chatting with sales staff, Managing Director Eric Thornton talked about what his sponsorship of Coulthard meant for him and his company. 'It was a straightforward business decision for us. It is not as if I or any of the directors are motor racing mad. But we believe that the range of trousers we produce for young people should be promoted by rising stars in sport, and David was one of the names we picked.' The sponsorship, reputedly around £50,000 a year, is a worthwhile investment, he feels: after every event like this, sales soar.

'When we first agreed the deal it was at the start of the 1994 season when he was driving in F3000. He was to model our trousers for some fashion shots, and turn up for a certain number of days during the year to events like this. Obviously now he has made it into F1 we could never even dream of affording the same sort of deal, but not only has he met all his commitments to us in full but you just need to ask him to do something and if it is humanly possible he does it. And he does it wholeheartedly. Turns up on time, meets people, is himself, and stays on for as long as people want him to.'

Shortly after this event Coulthard returned to Knockhill, the circuit where he had first driven a racing car just six years before, to meet with the Scottish press who had backed him from those early days. It was only 48 hours after news broke of the contractual battle, and the first time we had been able to talk to him. This was the biggest media gathering for a motorsport personality since the days of Jackie Stewart.

Reflecting on the fact that it was barely six months since he had been just another struggling F3000 driver with big hopes but virtually no budget, Coulthard was in typically forthright mood.

'Have you,' I asked, 'signed any sort of contract with McLaren?'

He was silent for the best part of half a minute. 'Jim, you are the first person I have admitted it to. Yes. But you all know me. You know I would not do anything dishonest. You know I would not have signed something unless I was sure I was legally entitled to do so.' He then explained with great conviction, how he would be doing a full season of F1 in 1995 with a top team, whichever one it was.

One thing about DC: ask him a straight question and you get a straight answer. The first time I met him was when he arrived in my office at *The Scotsman* early in 1989, shortly after David Leslie junior had tipped off the UK press about the potential of his new driver. Carrying the slim black attache case with the postage stamp size Saltire sticker which still accompanies him to this day, Coulthard sat down across the desk and explained that he was a racing driver and that he was going all the way. There was no rash talk of 'I'm the best' or 'I'm going into Formula 1' or the then current boast 'I'm going to be the next Jackie Stewart'. This was just a very confident, obviously determined 17-year-old boy sitting telling someone twice his age that he was going all the way. How right he was.

But back now to late 1994 and the contractual dispute. This would not be settled until after the season ended, and there were still three races to go. There was still the Nigel Mansell problem – and nobody underestimates Nigel Mansell in a race car, ever. Least of all Coulthard: If Nigel comes back and doesn't do very much then I'm in with a good

Right . . . *a Grand Prix concert with Eddie Irvine and Johnny Herbert* (ICN UK Bureau).

chance. *But if he is blindingly quick . . .* The young Scot did not need to speculate.

Mansell spun off in Jerez. He got bogged down behind Alesi in Suzuka, though he did show some of his old fire in the dreadful conditions. Then he went on to confront his own personal bogey, the street circuit of Adelaide. There, eight years earlier, the near certainty of his first World Championship became a 200 mph battle for life as his rear tyre exploded at the fastest part of the track. The result of the 1994 title fight ended just a whit less dramatically. Schumacher crashed into Hill, the only driver who could take the championship from him. Mansell, who had started from pole, but fallen nearly a minute behind, won the race.

Frank Williams is notoriously slow at making decisions. Here he was faced with a thorny dilemma. It was a choice between the man who had won more races for him than any other driver, or a 23-year-old newcomer who had not even raced for a full season. Williams might have gone either way: the Old Lionheart or the Young Pretender. It was as finely balanced as that. But there was that challenge from Ron Dennis and, perhaps more important, dissent within his own team. The message loud and clear on the jungle drums which reverberated through the team was *we do not want Nigel back.* Frank Williams gave his answer when he hired one of the UK's most accomplished – and expensive – advocates to argue, and easily win, his case in front of the FIA Contracts Recognition Board in Geneva.

The official announcement, originally scheduled for 1 January 1995, was delayed for a day to take into account the Scottish New Year. Nobody celebrates New Year like the Scots and, for one young Scot in particular, there really was something to celebrate. Coulthard, like thousands of other revellers, gathered outside the Tron Church in Edinburgh. It is, perhaps, one of the greatest street parties in Europe, one where the Scots really let their hair down and, some of them at least, get gloriously, uproariously drunk.

For Coulthard, 1995 already promised much. As a start, his basic income, he knew by now, was to increase ten-fold from around £50,000 a year to £500,000. On the strength of this he would move from his

Right *. . . checking on next year's vintage*
(ICN UK Bureau).

relatively humble house in Chiswick in central London, recently bought on the proceeds of his eight races with Williams, to a luxury flat overlooking the harbour in tax exile Monaco. It was the next logical step for the youngster who prided himself on having an organised life. Not that he was getting big-headed, or forgetting the recent cash flow struggles – but Monaco was where the big shots went.

Two days into 1995 Coulthard attended the hurriedly called press conference at Williams's Oxfordshire HQ. He was announced as the 'other' driver – the team stressed this, rather than calling him the number two driver – to partner Damon Hill.

Afterwards, following all the interviews, Coulthard toured the works and tried to talk to everyone in the place. It was the sort of gesture that some drivers might never have even thought of. For the Young Pretender, preparing to assume his countrymen's mantle, perhaps it was more than a New Year gesture, more a statement of faith.

You look after me guys, and I will look after you.

CHAPTER NINE

The new boy makes his mark

'IF THAT WAS a classic pole position lap by Schumacher,' said David Coulthard after the first qualifying session for the 1995 San Marino Grand Prix, 'then I think we can beat it.' This was a royal 'we', it should be noted, and referred to himself and not to any joint efforts by Coulthard and his Williams Renault team-mate Damon Hill.

Although Hill had won the previous race in Argentina, after Coulthard's car broke down while he was leading, the Scot already *knew* he could beat Hill. In the same race, just the second of his first full season in Formula 1, and only his tenth Grand Prix, he had proved to himself – after a brilliant overtaking manoeuvre that must have shaken Schumacher's confidence somewhat – that he was also well up to beating the German in a straight fight.

From a driver who exactly one year before had been no more than another young hopeful with a Formula 1 testing contract in his pocket, this dismissal of the World Champion in just 17 words might seem like supreme arrogance. But as Coulthard – the most dynamic new talent to enter F1 in years – observed after scoring the first podium position of his career by finishing second to Hill in the 1994 Portuguese Grand Prix, winning is all about confidence. 'Most of Schumacher's results come from his confidence. That is what makes the difference between winning and losing at this level of the sport.'

Coulthard's confidence before the start of the San Marino Grand Prix had never been higher. Until Schumacher's Benetton Renault lapped the heavily revised Imola circuit in one minute 27.274 seconds, and until Gerhard Berger in the Ferrari in front of a home crowd in the last minute of qualifying took provisional second spot with 1.27.282,

24-year-old Coulthard, the newest kid on the block, had dominated practice.

It was always going to be a dramatic Grand Prix. San Marino 1995 was Formula 1 staring at itself in the mirror and wondering if it liked what it saw. In 1994 both Roland Ratzenberger and Ayrton Senna had been killed at the same event. When the Formula 1 circus arrived this year – charged with emotion, and crowded by media persons eager to record every tearstain, every commemorative bouquet – what the sport, and the fans, wanted more than anything else was a good, fast, exciting race in which no-one got hurt. The race, it turned out, was all those things. Better still, it was won by Senna's team-mate Damon Hill on whom such a heavy burden had fallen after the triple World Champion's death.

Schumacher stormed off into the lead on wet tyres on a drying track, Berger – home favourite on a circuit just a few miles away from the Ferrari factory – was tracking him. Two seconds back sat David Coulthard, and behind him, showing no signs of wanting or indeed being able to force his way through, sat Damon Hill. Behind that, Jean Alesi in the second Ferrari. A long way back, in a completely different race, was Mika Hakkinen in sixth place and, somewhere beyond that, Nigel Mansell, the man who might have been at the wheel of Coulthard's car, a former World Champion making his long-awaited comeback to F1 in a McLaren Mercedes that had needed to be redesigned to accommodate his bulk.

Berger was first into the pits for the inevitable change to dry tyres and, within three laps, was the fastest man on the circuit by nearly two seconds a lap. Schumacher, racing a car that had been virtually rebuilt after a high-speed crash during second qualifying, angled the Benetton into the pits immediately after he heard the news on the pit-to-car radio, to fit dry tyres and take on fuel. Coulthard was now leading the race, the sixth he had led in his 11-race F1 career.

Some measure of the pressure on Schumacher comes from the fact that on his first flying lap with the new tyres he lost it, spun, spun again, hit the wall, spun, hit the wall again, and removed two wheels from the Benetton. Then there were only four drivers up front. Hill, who had also heard the news about Berger on dry tyres, was leaving the pits when Schumacher crashed. Coulthard was just coming in for what would turn out to be a slightly slower stop. When the race settled, two

David and Damon. If Hill ever expected the young Scot to play the dutiful number two driver, he was in for a series of shocks.

After his earnings jumped ten-fold when he signed full-time for Williams Renault for 1995, business manager Tim Wright became indispensable.

Unveiling the FW17 and its drivers.

laps later, Berger led from Hill, Alesi climbing all over the rear of Coulthard in third place. This was what F1 was all about, what the fans had come to see.

When Berger came in for fuel on the 21st lap he stalled the engine, took vital seconds to restart and then there were three – Hill, Coulthard, and Alesi. For Hill in the lead, there was some comfort to be drawn from the fact that, although Coulthard was in his wheel tracks, the sole team order stated that the two team-mates must not take each other off. So while Coulthard was free to pass him, if he could, he must not force his way through and risk a crash.

Like him or loathe him, the new kid on the block was determined, quick, and driving a fast car

---

Alesi, swarming all over the back of Coulthard's car, could, perhaps would, do anything he needed to get past. Alesi, driving the legendary number 27 Ferrari, the man who had catapulted to fame by, however briefly, passing Ayrton Senna in the Canadian Grand Prix five years before, had more than 80 races under his belt without a win. He was a desperate man in a marque desperate for a win, especially at home.

Coulthard, under tremendous pressure from Alesi – even occasionally banging wheels – tracked his team-mate, always looking for the way through, always trying to hold the Ferrari at bay as the three weaved through the backmarkers. But Coulthard was playing his own game. It was a game he had been playing since making his debut in kart racing at the age of 12.

On lap 25 Alesi pulled into the pits and Coulthard really piled on the pressure. Then, tucked just too closely under the leader's rear wing, he lost it, spun on the Villeneuve curve, quickly recovered and set off again after Hill. With his scheduled pit stop due any minute, the Scot went straight in for fuel and a change of tyres, his old ones covered in gravel. When he emerged, and leader Hill rejoined after his second stop, there were just seven seconds between them. Alesi, in the leading Ferrari, was another seven seconds behind.

In his anxiety for a fast stop, however, the young Scot had broken the 120 kph speed limit in the pit lane. An electronic speed limiter, one that the drivers can select to ensure that their cars remain below the

120 kph limit, was fitted to all cars after the previous year's Imola race following an incident when four mechanics were hurt. 'I had selected the limiter in first gear, then I changed into second to prevent wheelspin. Before I could engage the limiter in second gear I had broken the speed limit. I sort of hoped I might get away with it, but they caught me and called me in.'

He was called in for a 10-second stop/go penalty which helped cost him the race. The result would now be between Hill and Alesi. Coulthard apparently would have to settle for third place, with Berger a distant fourth. Unknown to the Scot, however, a kerb had damaged the endplate on the front wing of the Williams and when he was called in to have this replaced just 20 laps from the end, he lost nearly half a minute, letting Berger through into third.

And that, it turned out, was the story of the 1995 San Marino Grand Prix. The racing was fast, tempers were at times furious, no-one had been even slightly hurt, and F1 could look forward to the future with guarded optimism. Furthermore, the season promised genuine competition in store. No fewer than five drivers (Hill, Schumacher, Berger, Alesi and Coulthard) and three teams (Williams, Benetton and Ferrari) were in with a chance of the drivers' and constructors' titles. In 1994 there had been only three drivers (Senna, Schumacher and Hill) and two teams (Williams and Benetton). The two years before that, there had been only one driver (Prost in 1993, Mansell in 1992) and one team (Williams) with a realistic hope.

After the race Coulthard admitted, 'today I just made too many mistakes, first spinning, then speeding in the pits.' Jean Alesi – notoriously difficult to pass on the circuit, and a man whose utterings can be as fiery and undisciplined as his driving style – turned on the Scot with the sort of back-handed compliment that, from him, confirms that a new driver has really arrived in Formula 1. 'I have had good battles with lots of other drivers,' spat the French Sicilian after the race, 'but he is one of the most incorrect drivers I have ever seen.' Coulthard remained cool. 'I don't know what Alesi was complaining about. It was a good race. That is what racing is all about after all.'

Others have commented on Coulthard's desperate but highly skilled defensive battle with Alesi. Either way, there was no doubting that, like him or loathe him, the new kid on the block was determined, quick, and driving a fast car. Courageous too. Looking forward to the next race, in Spain, he said: 'I am very confident now because I am on the pace and I know so much more about Formula 1 than I did when I turned up for my first race there last year. Then I knew absolutely zero. If I had realised that then, I would have been a lot more nervous!'

Coulthard has been demonstrating his agility since the very start of the 1995 season in Brazil. Right from first practice.

On the Friday, in the first timed practice session for the Brazilian Grand Prix, Damon Hill took his Williams Renault round the 2.7 mile Interlagos circuit in one minute 21.664 seconds. It was the fastest time. Damon Hill was very definitely hot. Even as Hill backed off and relaxed on his slowing down lap, David Coulthard lapped the same circuit in one minute 21.666 seconds, just two thousandths of a second slower. Schumacher was third fastest – nearly a whole second a lap slower.

For Coulthard, just three days away from his 24th birthday, it was the latest confirmation that he had well and truly arrived in F1. It was also a warning, should his team-mate need one, that the much publicised power struggles between them the previous season were going to be a fact of life, however urbane relations might now seem to be, as expressed to the media. To put the lap into some sort of context, it was not only the first time Coulthard had ever driven on the South American continent, never mind the circuit, and it came after a week of suffering with tonsilitis which had prevented him completing the gruelling daily regime a Formula 1 driver needs to undergo just to be able to drive the car, never mind race it.

This first race of the new season was always going to be sensational. The circuit is near Sao Paulo, Ayrton Senna's home town. Emotions ran high for the Brazilians, still openly mourning the loss of their national hero, whose death had given the young Williams test driver his opening as an F1 racing driver.

In Friday's first official practice session Damon Hill, perhaps not surprisingly, set fastest time with a lap of one minute 20.081 seconds. Second fastest – albeit nearly a second adrift – was Gerhard Berger, again not surprisingly knowing both his skill and Ferrari's history of doing well whenever there is an engine capacity change (this year from 3.5 litres to 3 litres) in Formula 1. Coulthard, struggling with massive understeer, was three-tenths of a second behind the Austrian, but still nearly one second a lap faster than Michael Schumacher.

The World Champion, going into one of the fastest corners of his fastest lap, suffered a steering failure which he would subsequently blame on the bumpiness of the circuit. Despite having been completely resurfaced since the last Grand Prix the track was so bad that even Rubens Barrichello, the new local hero, called for it to be ripped up and relaid before the 1996 race.

The terror of a steering failure in a racing car cannot be over-emphasised, not least because that is believed to have been the reason behind Ayrton Senna's fatal crash. If the brakes fail at speed the driver can use the steering and throttle to spin the car to a halt. If a tyre blows the driver retains control over throttle, steering and brakes. If the throttle sticks open he can use the engine cut-out, brakes and steering to bring the car to a halt. If the steering goes the driver becomes a helpless passenger in an unguided missile.

Schumacher was lucky. After the car halted he jumped out, leapt on to a tyre barrier – and pondered just what the hell was going on. Later,

Coulthard with his Canadian girlfriend Andrea Murray (ICN UK Bureau).

he told his team in no uncertain terms that either the problem was fixed, or he was out of Sunday's race. Schumacher's mechanics worked until 5 am the next day to fix the steering. Schumacher would, of course, race.

In the second qualifying session on Saturday afternoon Schumacher crashed again, but not until he had set second fastest time of the day behind Damon Hill. Hill had not improved on his Friday time but Schumacher did, so did Coulthard. So too did Johnny Herbert in the second Benetton. The Ferraris were fifth and sixth.

In the early morning warm-up on race day, Coulthard was fastest. In the chronology of a Grand Prix – which before 1997, when one-day qualifying was introduced, began with the first untimed session on the Friday and continued until the chequered flag dropped – this can sometimes be significant, sometimes not. In theory at least, warm-up is the first time the drivers run the cars in race trim set-up for two reliable hours rather than four laps of speed. Sometimes, however, it is no more than another chance to psyche the opposition by heading the all-important time sheets. The time sheets, issued after every time the cars go out on race weekend, analyse their performance to one thousandth of a second, only one thousandth of one kilometre per hour. Top of the sheets is the only place to be – and where Coulthard was on race day morning in Brazil.

As the cars lined up on the grid on Sunday afternoon, with everyone hoping this opening race would herald the start of a happier, less controversial season, it seemed that Formula 1 was still not free of the swarm of technical troubles that had plagued the sport last year. A fuel sample supplied by Elf for the Renault engines of both Williams and Benetton had failed pre-race scrutineering in Brazil despite having passed scrutiny in Europe by the FIA, the sport's governing body. The results of the race would therefore only be provisional for any drivers with Renault engines who finished. Some drivers were informed of the situation by their team before the start. David Coulthard was not.

But as the 26 Formula 1 cars lined up on the dummy grid, the biggest thing on most drivers' minds was surviving the first corner which, whether you are a 12-year-old kart racer or a 42-year-old Formula 1

Right *Brazil, 1995. Getting ready for his first timed session on a track he'd never seen, on a continent where he'd never been before, and him still recovering from tonsillitis.*

The start of the race . . . (ICN UK Bureau)

veteran, is always the most dangerous moment of your life. They all survived, Schumacher outdragging Hill to the first corner, Coulthard slotting in behind his team-mate, Herbert getting lost, Hakkinen flying, Alesi out-accelerating Berger, then Irvine, Katayama and Salo in less than the blink of an eye.

Within a couple of laps it became obvious there were only three cars in the race, Schumacher and Hill, then Coulthard stalking, a couple of seconds back but pulling away from Hakkinen, watching, waiting for a mistake from the front two. On lap four Hill attacked Schumacher, nearly got through, was forced to back off and, in the scrabbling, off-line recovery nearly lost second place as Coulthard pounced, drew alongside and nearly, *nearly* got past. But it was too early for such a risk. Next lap order, Schumacher, Hill, then Coulthard, then, after a bigger gap, Hakkinen, then the rest.

That was the pattern for the early part of the race. Hill harrying Schumacher, Coulthard five seconds back. 'I could not keep up their pace so I backed off and decided to run at a comfortable lap time,' he said. The three of them were all the time pulling away from Hakkinen and the rest. Gerhard Berger was a distant fifth, not that it seemed to matter.

Schumacher came in early on lap 18 for the first of what was obviously going to be three pit stops. For four laps Hill led before coming in for his first stop followed, one lap later, by the Scot. The Williams Renault pair favoured a two-stop strategy. Hill came out fast, ahead of Schumacher, and that seemed to be it on a track where there are very few passing opportunities. Then, on lap 20, Hill had trouble with the automatic gearbox. On the next lap he had serious trouble changing down and the car spun. The transmission troubles and bad luck which had dogged Coulthard's 1994 season from his very first race, and which had denied him at least one victory, were suddenly Hill's troubles.

Now it was a two-car race, Coulthard tracking Schumacher. The rest, still led by Hakkinen, were more than half a minute back and drifting away. On lap 35 Schumacher pulled in for his second stop. Coulthard took the lead and started to try to tease out enough of a gap to let him make his second stop and emerge close enough behind Schumacher to guarantee he would be first when the German exited the pits for the

. . . and a good start to the season. Coulthard was the only driver to finish on the same lap as Michael Schumacher. It was a victory that turned temporarily sour, however – except for Gerhard Berger (ICN UK Bureau).

third time. But it was not to be. Even with only a dozen survivors, and both Schumacher and Coulthard lapping everyone else on the circuit, the Brazilian Grand Prix came down, quite simply, to traffic. Gerhard Berger, who was to finish third, a whole lap behind, appeared to be very helpful when Schumacher came up to lap him. When Coulthard arrived, he appeared less so.

After the race, after the national anthems and the flag waving and the champagne spraying, the three drivers arrived in the press room for the post-race interview which is broadcast all over the world. But as they took their places in front of the media and began the other post-race ritual of downing large quantities of mineral water, Bob Constanduros, who traditionally fronts these interviews, congratulated the drivers – but added the bombshell that the results were only provisional in view of a possible irregularity with the fuel of the Benetton number 1 and Williams number 6 cars.

Coulthard, who had not been warned of the potential fuel problem before the race, was livid

Schumacher, upon whose face one can normally read every emotion, appeared indifferent. Coulthard, who had arrived beaming, looked as though someone had punched him somewhere very precious. Gerhard Berger, ever the joker, was delighted. 'No, no, the protest stands, they are disqualified.' Everyone except Schumacher and Coulthard laughed. Good old Berger.

The fuel samples supplied by Elf, and approved by the FIA in Europe were not, according to officials at the track, legal. The thought of Elf, oldest continuous fuel supplier in F1, cheating seemed simply out of the question. The thought of the FIA bungling, again, did not. Schumacher and Coulthard were for the moment disqualified. The outcome of a vigorous appeal by both Benetton and Williams would have to wait until after the Argentinian Grand Prix two weeks later. Coulthard, who had not been warned of potential problems with the fuel before the start of the race, was livid. 'They should,' he said quietly, 'have told me.'

The mental and physical build up to the 1995 Argentinian Grand Prix, first in that country for 14 years, began just three hours after the end of the Brazilian race with the madcap escape from the circuit. No-one, save possibly Brazilian drivers, can stand the Brazilian Grand Prix, especially in Sao Paulo.

It is a rough, tough, nasty place where, unless you are one of the handful of super rich, you could not possibly want to live. Visitors, most of whom are drawn by the Grand Prix, want nothing more than to get through the journeys from the airport to the track to the airport and the days in between, and hope that their car does not break down. If they are on their own, and their car does break down, they hope that the end comes quickly. Bob Constanduros puts it succinctly. 'If you survive Sao Paulo, if your hire car keeps going, if your hotel is OK, if your communications work, if you get your story across, all without trouble, then you know that the rest of the year is going to be a good one.'

The fastest way out of Sao Paulo after the race is on the 9.30 pm British Airways flight to London Heathrow. You leave Brazil in the middle of the night and arrive in London around noon. The difference between the two countries, even to experienced travellers, is as obvious as night and day. At the airport, queuing to get on the plane, Coulthard looks pleased with himself, despite the fuel row.

'What about the World Championship?' I ask him.

'I don't want to think about the World Championship until I have won a Grand Prix,' he replies.

But the idea had obviously occurred to him, the very audacity of the thought that he could have a serious go at winning the World Championship in his first full season of Formula 1 (and if so of challenging Emerson Fittipaldi's record as youngest World Champion, winning the title in 1972 aged 25 years, eight months).

A fortnight later, in the pouring wet of the first practice for the Argentinian Grand Prix, David Coulthard grabbed provisional pole with a lap more than one second faster than his team-mate Damon Hill could manage. Third fastest was Schumacher, two-tenths of a second behind Hill. On the Saturday, in the final qualifying session in which most drivers waited until the final 10 minutes before venturing out on to the drying track, Damon Hill came back with two fast laps on the trot, either of them, he thought, good enough to guarantee him pole position for the race.

As he eased his Williams into the pit lane garage at the end of his stint, Hill sat back to watch the results of his rivals on the small monitor the mechanics placed on the bodywork in front of his face. Above it, he could see the rain starting to fall on the other side of the track, ready to obliterate the marginally dry line which had given him his time. With just seconds remaining in the final qualifying session, Coulthard bullied and cajoled his sliding, slithering Williams car round the Argentinian circuit eight-tenths of a second faster than his team-mate. He had won the first pole position start of his Formula 1 career. Almost unnoticed, Michael Schumacher performed similar heroics to cement third place on the starting grid.

On the Sunday morning warm-up, on the first dry track of the weekend, Coulthard was a disappointing fifth fastest behind Hill, Berger, Alesi, and Schumacher. If he was at all worried, it did not show. He had, after all, been fastest in the warm-up in Brazil – for all the good it had done him.

As Coulthard led the parade lap of a Grand Prix for the first time in his life, and in only his tenth appearance, the pressure must have felt immense. With Damon Hill starting alongside him, the World Champion immediately behind, Eddie Irvine alongside him and another 22 ambitious drivers lined up behind them, the risk of making a mistake at the start seemed extremely high.

Coulthard made a perfect start. Hill slotted in behind, Schumacher behind that. Beyond them the grid had gone mad. Jean Alesi, fighting for his career, skidded and felt his Ferrari tapped from behind going into the first corner. In the resulting chaos five cars were destroyed. The race was red-flagged to a halt at the end of the opening lap. Four drivers – Alesi, Hakkinen, Barrichello and Herbert – grabbed their custom-made seats from their cars and rushed back to the pits. They knew that the spare cars were awaiting them. Barrichello, dramatically shorter than team-mate Eddie Irvine, for whom the spare car had been set up, would not quite make his grid position for the second start. He started from the back of the grid. The fifth driver, Bertrand Gachot in a Pacific, had no spare car.

The second start to the first Argentinian Grand Prix in 14 years simply doubled the pressure on Coulthard who, like every pole position man before him, had to summon every ounce of his concentration and willpower not to lose the crucially important advantage so hard won in qualifying.

In Argentina, Coulthard led from pole at both the start and the restart and was running away with the race until throttle problems put him out after just 16 laps.

However he received the first Carlitos Menem Memorial Trophy from the President of Argentina. The trophy is now presented each year to the pole position winner, in memory of the President's late son, a rally driver, who was killed in a helicopter crash on the way to an event (ICN UK Bureau).

San Marino Grand Prix. One minute's silence in memory of Ayrton Senna (ICN UK Bureau).

127

Coulthard made no mistake. Hill, his car hesitating for just a fraction of a second, did. When the cars crossed the line at the end of the first lap Coulthard was two seconds clear of Schumacher. Hill was swarming all over the German's gearbox. Six laps into the race and Coulthard was driving away, now four seconds clear with Hill still swarming fruitlessly over the Benetton. Then, on lap six, as he cleared the first hairpin after the finishing straight, the electrics on Coulthard's car suddenly died.

The Scot coasted round the corner losing vital seconds. But, just as the Schumacher-Hill combination appeared in his mirrors, the Williams Renault came back to life. Coulthard, finding the car suddenly alive, grabbed first gear, and left long strips of rubber on the tarmac as he sought to get back up to speed. But Schumacher and Hill were through. He was down to third. Three laps later there were three cars contesting the lead – Schumacher, Hill, Coulthard – passing as fast as you could say their names. On the next lap Hill ducked inside Schumacher and was gone. Coulthard, desperate to catch his team-mate, first had to pass the World Champion. After the Brazilian Grand Prix he had told me, 'sure, Michael is quick, but he can be beaten'.

All het up, he really lit the fires and started to pull away – then the electrics died

---

On the fourteenth lap Coulthard was tucked right up under Schumacher's rear wing as he completed the lap, his car sliding all over the road as he traded downforce for closeness. Ahead of Schumacher, just two car lengths away, was the Minardi Ford of Pierluigi Martini.

On to the start-finish straight and as Schumacher slipstreamed the Minardi ready to take Martini at the end of the straight Coulthard, coming like a train, ducked right. Schumacher moved right to block him. Coulthard, travelling slightly faster, ducked left and drew alongside. Schumacher, on the inside line, might still win the corner. Then the Scot stayed off the brakes longer, twisted his car to the right, in front of Schumacher and inside the Minardi and, in one of the best overtaking manoeuvres seen in F1 for years, he was in front of Martini and Schumacher was behind. For Coulthard, it was the chance to go hunting for Hill, now 10 seconds in front. For Schumacher it was perhaps the most devastating blow to his confidence he had experienced in Formula 1.

On lap 16 Hill pitted, took a leisurely 15.5 seconds, and emerged in third place. Coulthard, all het up, really lit the fires. He started to pull away. He lasted just two more laps. On the first corner after starting his seventeenth lap, the electrics died. The Williams rolled off the track and on to the grass.

After parking the car, and watching Schumacher retake the lead, the Scot sat for long, long seconds reflecting on his luck. In the adrenalin high from which his body would take hours to recover, it is doubtful if he would have been able to sit and reason it out beyond the abysmal disappointment of not finishing another race. Yet everyone who had watched the race knew the truth. The 1995 World Championship was now at least a three-horse race.

By the time Damon Hill crossed the line to take his tenth F1 victory nearly one and a half hours later, Jean Alesi had confirmed that Ferrari were back in the hunt, and Gerhard Berger led the title race with 11 points to Damon Hill's 10. Michael Schumacher, nearly half a minute behind Hill, had the appearance of a broken man.

The post-fuel row Brazilian results at that stage still stood. It was not until the following week that the FIA decided to overturn the disqualification of Schumacher and Coulthard, reinstating them as winner and runner-up respectively of the Brazilian Grand Prix. The drivers had their points restored, moving the German into the lead in the Drivers' Championship with 14 points, ahead of Damon Hill with 10 points, Jean Alesi with eight, and David Coulthard fourth with six points. However the Constructors' points were not restored to the Benetton and Williams teams, whose punishment also included a hefty fine.

A poignant postscript to the Argentinian Grand Prix. Coulthard received the first Carlitos Menem Memorial Trophy, now presented to the pole position winner each year in memory of the only son of the Argentine President. The 26-year-old rally driver was killed in a helicopter crash a month before the GP when travelling to a competition.

• CHAPTER TEN •

Countdown
to victory

AS COULTHARD BEGAN his preparations for the fourth race of the 1995 season in Spain, another factor came into play, one that would affect his performance in the next three Grands Prix to the extent that it almost certainly cost him his job at Williams. The tonsillitis which had plagued him throughout the closed season was back, with a vengeance. Tonsillitis is normally associated with children. Like so many ailments that young patients seem to shrug off with ease, it has a much greater impact on an adult, and particularly on a superfit adult whose body is honed into otherwise perfect physical condition. The solution, a tonsillectomy, was not possible immediately. Coulthard simply could not tell Frank Williams he would have to take time out: in the mind of a young driver in his first full season in the best car in the world that was never even up for consideration.

The next races – Spain, Monaco, and Canada – were a complete washout for the Scot who, immediately after returning from Montreal, booked himself into a private clinic in Oxfordshire for the operation. For the French Grand Prix, his first at Magny-Cours (Nigel Mansell having guested for Williams the year before) Coulthard was feeling better than he had done for months but acknowledged he was still not back to full fitness.

He was fit enough however to qualify in third place behind Hill and Schumacher who by now were in their own two-horse race for the World Championship. No matter what the cause of individual failures, after five races without an appearance on the podium the Scot knew that his job was on the line, so it was no surprise that he was happy to come home a comfortable third and leave the two championship contenders to battle it out ahead of him.

That battle became a physical one at Silverstone when Hill, desperate to overtake Schumacher for a home win, crashed into the back of the German's Benetton and took them both off. Coulthard, who had been dropped to fifth by his second pit stop, was easily hauling in the Ferrari of Jean Alesi and the Benetton of Johnny Herbert who could hardly believe his luck to be suddenly leading his home event.

As he passed the parked cars of the leaders Coulthard suddenly woke up, realised he was on for a win, and put the foot down. The next few laps, as he dispatched Alesi then Herbert, were among the most spectacular in his Formula 1 career to date. Herbert, however, argued later that by the time Coulthard was close enough to pass he already knew something that the Scot did not, and made no attempt to resist.

In his haste to rejoin the race Coulthard had, the pit lane officials insisted, broken the 75mph speed limit within the pit lane. A ten second stop/go penalty was the result. Quite what happened has never been fully explained, least of all by the driver. One favourite theory among the pit lane gossips was that the Scot had been penalised because, with Hill and Schumacher out, it would be politic if another driver and car combination won the event. Coulthard himself simply accepted the fact and got on with the job.

On the podium he and Alesi picked up Herbert and held him aloft in one of the few scenes of genuine affection seen in the sport for decades.

Two consecutive third places might be a dream result for many young drivers but for Coulthard, knowing that victory had been virtually handed to him on a plate, it was nothing like good enough. Ominously, Frank Williams obviously agreed. By the time the Grand Prix circus turned up at Hockenheim it was being whispered that the Scot was almost certainly going to be replaced in 1996 by French Canadian Jacques Villeneuve, son of the legendary Ferrari driver Giles, winner of the gruelling Indianapolis 500 and, aged 24, soon to be crowned the youngest IndyCar Champion in more than four decades.

But if Coulthard was supposed to be worried he certainly did not show it.

Overleaf *A cool eye and a firm hand. Coulthard was a force to be reckoned with in 1995* (The Scotsman and ICN UK Bureau).

Three months previously Nigel Mansell, who had been bribed and coaxed into a McLaren Mercedes in one of the most unlikely alliances in the history of the sport, had stepped from the uncompetitive red and white car at the Spanish Grand Prix after just four races with his new team and stalked off into retirement.

Although Mark Blundell and Jan Magnussen would try (and fail) to make Mansell's car work before the season was finished, Coulthard already had an understanding with McLaren team owner Ron Dennis for the following year, and so it would prove – but not before a late season burst of rumours which even had the Scot pencilled in to join Michael Schumacher at Ferrari.

As his team-mate Damon Hill leads the pack around the St. Devote bend at the start of the 1995 Monaco Grand Prix, Coulthard flies through the air after rubbing tyres with Jean Alesi. The race was restarted following the subsequent crash which involved many cars (Popperfoto/Reuter).

All hands to the pump (ICN UK Bureau).

That was all in the future, however. There was still the German Grand Prix to be run and almost half the season to go.

Hill and Schumacher, as had become inevitable, dominated the front row of the grid, with Coulthard third. Hill got away cleanly but then, well ahead of Schumacher as he approached the last corner on the first lap, he lost it and drove straight on into the gravel trap. The German crowd, already baying for a Schumacher home win, were ecstatic. When Coulthard made no attempt to catch their hero they went delirious. Frank Williams, witnessing his team's humiliation from the pit lane, felt pretty emotional too. That afternoon, any doubts about Villeneuve replacing the Scot vanished.

Coulthard, a safe second place assured, had his own agenda. After whiteouts in Spain, Monaco and Canada he wanted World

Championship points. Third place in the championship was the only option left for him. It was something he had to do. He also had to win a race. Next year, he might not be driving the best car in the world. Germany proved to be the turning point. Fully recovered physically, and mentally boosted by his hat-trick of podium finishes, he felt he had enough title points in the bag to go for it. Each race became a battle for pole with team-mate Hill, to the point that Schumacher and the rest were virtually banned from the front row for the rest of the year.

In Hungary Hill took pole, got away cleanly and led the Scot all the way to the flag. At Spa the Williams pair had an off day, Coulthard qualifying 5th, Hill eighth. In the race Coulthard's gearbox let go after 13 laps and he was out. Hill struggled home a distant second behind Schumacher. The only thing the Scot took away from Belgium was the knowledge that he could, and he had, out qualified his team-mate.

He knew he could win pole and keep the lead from pole – winning was surely just a matter of time

---

At the Italian Grand Prix Coulthard out qualified Hill again but this time it was for pole position, his second in Formula 1. Leading the pack round Monza on the parade lap, however, Coulthard's dream debut in front turned into a nightmare, and one that could hardly have been more public. At the exit to the Ascari chicane, an artificial corner put there to drag down lap times and, in theory at least, make racing safer, he spun off the road and into the gravel. It was a major blow. With the car damaged and out of the race, the Scot began the long walk back to the pits to explain to Frank Williams and Patrick Head how no, he hadn't simply given the throttle an over-exuberant prod while showing off to the fanatical Italians.

The race, meanwhile, started without him and continued to exactly the same spot where his Williams had spun off. This time, however, half the field spun off. The race was red-flagged. Maybe it wasn't his fault after all. Maybe the dream was still on. The red flag meant a new race – Coulthard could retake the start from pole position, using the spare car. This time he made no mistake. Just 13 laps into the race, however, with the Scot running away with it, a front wheel bearing collapsed and spun the car on to the gravel. Coulthard nursed it back to the pits and retirement. Later, much later in the race, Hill crashed into Schumacher and took both of them out. Johnny Herbert inherited the second win of his career.

But Coulthard now knew he could win pole position, he knew too that he could keep the lead from pole. A win from pole position was only a matter of time, surely?

The Portuguese Grand Prix, 13th of the season, was to prove lucky at last. Hill was fastest in the Friday qualifying after getting his car sorted out earlier with a lap of 1.21.322, less than a tenth of a second ahead of Coulthard but more than half a second ahead of Schumacher's Benetton in third place. On Saturday, with his car working better and perfect conditions, Coulthard pushed and moved into the one minute 20s, securing pole with 1.20.537. Hill, the only other driver to get into the 1.20s, could not get nearer than 1.20.905 – nearly half a second back. Nor was it for lack of trying. Hill knew that Schumacher was the only one who could get near the Williams cars, and that pole position would put him directly ahead of the German on the grid. It is immeasurably more difficult to pass the car starting immediately in front to one on the opposite side of the track.

But that was not to be. The order was Coulthard, Hill, Schumacher and Berger, followed by Frentzen, Herbert, Alesi and Barrichello. As Coulthard led the pack away on the parade lap, everyone watched and wondered if the farce in Monza would be replayed. It was not. Nor was there any mistake at the start. Not from Coulthard, not from Hill, not from Schumacher – they all got away in the order in which they started.

Behind them, however, the grid had gone mad. Martin Brundle's Ligier tapped Frentzen's Sauber into a spin and sent Barrichello off the track to avoid a worse crash. Further back there were even bigger problems as Katayama's Tyrrell inexplicably swerved into the Minardi of Luca Badoer sending the Japanese driver's car into a series of barrel rolls. The red flag came out and the drivers had to start all over again.

Coulthard, under immense pressure at having to beat the two title contenders off the start line for a second time, made no mistake. His team-mate did though and the wily Schumacher angled the Benetton into second spot as the pack reached the first corner. Schumacher on your gearbox is the ultimate nightmare for any race driver, whatever they may say in public and, even with Coulthard on form, it was easy to surmise that the German would get ahead and drive away, with the

Scot very decently easing over to let Hill take up the chase.

Except that no-one had told the Scot. Coulthard simply stormed away from the Benetton on the first lap. On the second he set what would be the fastest lap of the race. The effort wasn't reckless, it was cool-headed, clear, considered. Establish the ground rules early on, pull away on the opening laps, break the opposition. It was the classic Senna tactic.

As Coulthard disappeared Hill became trapped behind Schumacher, his world title hopes beginning to fade. For Schumacher, merely to finish ahead of Hill would effectively cement his lead. For Hill nothing less than ten points for a win would do if he was to reduce the 17-point deficit.

Behind Hill there was an increasing gap to the Benetton of Berger who led the rest of the pack. While Coulthard was comfortably pulling out enough of a lead to allow him to pit for fuel and tyres and resume ahead of the pack, Schumacher and Hill both pitted early. Schumacher's stop was a slick seven second affair. Hill's was terrible. He was stationary for more than 16 seconds, struggling to engage first gear.

'Now this is the way to do it, laddie . . .' A word of advice from mentor Jackie Stewart (ICN UK Bureau).

And maybe it worked. Coulthard came second in Hungary, behind team-mate Hill, but ahead of veteran racer Gerhard Berger . . . (ICN UK Bureau)

Two laps later Coulthard peeled off, stopped for a leisurely but safe ten seconds, roared onto the track four seconds ahead of Schumacher and immediately began to tease out a lead once more. His case was helped by the fact that Hill was stuck behind a truculent Alesi on worn tyres, losing three seconds a lap and letting Schumacher build an advantage. This and the pit stop cost him any chance of a win.

Coulthard, as he approached half distance and his second stop, faced a similar problem. Though he dismissed the tail-runners with arrogant disdain, getting through the midfielders promised some grief, enough perhaps to let Schumacher, just seven seconds back, close in thanks to his mastery in traffic.

No way. The gap between the two leaders barely moved.

At exactly half distance Schumacher flitted into the pits, paused for 7.5 seconds and was away. One lap later Coulthard did the same thing and needed four seconds longer. It was a slow stop, but fast enough to get him out in front of the Benetton. But not in front of Hill. The Englishman, wrongfooted into thinking that Schumacher had chosen a two stop strategy, had changed his plan to two stops and was struggling on worn tyres. He led for just five laps, his team-mate climbing all over him, before pitting for his final stop.

Hill was still not finished and when Coulthard and Schumacher pitted for their third and final stops, Coulthard this time losing two seconds but again keeping the lead, the Englishman moved into second spot. With fresher tyres, however, Schumacher simply took a couple of laps to choose his spot then, with nine laps to go, he dived down the inside on the tight uphill right-hand corner added to the track as a safety measure after Senna's death and was through. Just.

With eight laps to go and an eight-second lead, some drivers might

. . . and got his maiden F1 victory three races later in Portugal despite a dramatic start, then a restart. Schumacher and Hill enjoyed the celebrations too (ICN UK Bureau).

Overleaf *Poleman Coulthard led the start of both the European and Pacific Grands Prix* (ICN UK Bureau).

have panicked at the thought of Schumacher on the charge. But the Scot stayed calm and the German could only close by one second before Coulthard crossed the line, both hands in the air, to record his all-important first Grand Prix victory.

This was the perfect result. Pole, fastest lap, victory. And it was made all the more sweet, all the more weighty, because he won it against the best in the world. None of his rivals had mechanical problems, fell off or blundered in any way. 'It's getting to the back end of the year, and it was important for me to win a race while I had the opportunity. You never know how competitive different cars are going to be next year.' It came as little surprise that he dedicated the win to his family, specifically to his parents Duncan and Joyce, who had backed him all the way from those very first days in karting.

There were now four races to go. Coulthard knew that winning again might not be an option, with Hill still intent on denying Schumacher a second consecutive world title.

At the Nurburgring, for the European Grand Prix, the Scot took his

Frank Williams seemed to respect Coulthard's approach, but not enough to retain him for 1996, despite his third position in the 1995 Drivers' Championship (ICN UK Bureau).

There were some people however who never doubted that he would make it to the very top – Coulthard with his parents Joyce and Duncan (Scottish Daily Record).

third pole position in a row and led on a rapidly drying track until Alesi, on slicks, stormed through followed by Schumacher. Coulthard let Hill by to chase the World Championship leader but the Englishman tried just too hard to pass the Ferrari, damaged the nose of the Williams and was forced to retire.

Schumacher won, Alesi second, Coulthard a distant third.

On his first trip to Aida for the Pacific Grand Prix – postponed because of a major earthquake earlier in the year – the Scot took his fourth consecutive pole from Hill who was still desperately trying to catch Schumacher. The Scot led going away and was 13 seconds clear by lap 10. Buoyed by his lead he decided to abandon his planned three-stop strategy and go for two instead, in the hope that the time saved by not stopping, plus his lead, would cushion him from Schumacher and

Hill who were temporarily stuck behind Berger's Ferrari. It nearly worked. Coulthard beat Hill but Schumacher's slick pit routines were enough to get him past Coulthard at the final stops securing, in the process, his second consecutive world title.

At Suzuka the following week the newly crowned champion dominated the Japanese race, taking pole position, fastest lap and the flag. The Williams had started with Hill in fourth position, Coulthard in sixth. In the wet race the Scot spun off at the notorious Spoon curve, Hill followed him at the same corner, just one lap later. 'It was not one of our better days,' said Williams technical director Patrick Head.

Coulthard's first race in Australia was also to be his last for Williams, Nigel Mansell having taken his place, and won, the year before. Though he lost pole by a fraction to Hill he had a cunning plan for the start. 'I walked the course before the race and looked carefully at the kerbs on the outside of the first corner. I reckoned you could bounce the car on them if you took the outside line and that would get you past whoever was on the inside, pole position line.'

It worked exactly to plan, the sheer audacity of it provoking Hill to swarm all over his team-mate's rear wing. Hill could not get past and pitted on lap 19 hoping to make up time with a fast stop. It took 9.6 seconds but it did not really matter. Coming in for his stop, on the following lap, Coulthard peeled into the pit lane, slowed for the first hairpin corner and ploughed straight on into the pit wall.

After the race, which Hill went on to win, there were muttered excuses from, and for, Coulthard – jammed throttle, oil on the track, tickover speed too high. But nothing could take away from the fact that this was an ignominious end to what had been a promising season.

• CHAPTER ELEVEN •

New team, new problems

WHEN COULTHARD OFFICIALLY reported for duty at McLaren International's impressive Woking HQ early in 1996 he was well aware that, after his debut seasons at Williams driving what everyone acknowledged was the best car in the sport, the sweat and toil of Formula 1 was about to begin in earnest. The Mercedes-powered McLaren, with its distinctive third wing situated above the driver's airbox to give added downforce, had been the most public of failures following Nigel Mansell's highly emotive retirement from the sport early the previous season. Work was well in hand for a modified design to begin the new season but it was, as yet, unproven.

As well as an uncompetitive car, the Scot faced the considerable bond between Ron Dennis and Finnish driver Mika Hakkinen who had, many believed, filled a void in Dennis's life following the death of Ayrton Senna.

Hakkinen had effectively put his own life on the line too during a high-speed accident in qualifying for the Australian Grand Prix at the end of the previous season, spending several days in a coma. It was a crash from which many feared he might not be able to make it back.

Although Dennis had been keen to sign Coulthard, even to the extent of testing the Scot's Williams contract in the courts, Hakkinen was the established star, his favourite. With one Grand Prix win to his credit against none for the Finn, and with third place in the 1995 drivers' championship to Hakkinen's seventh, Coulthard had plenty of confidence. But it was always going to be a difficult situation. Hakkinen was very much the same era as Coulthard yet the two had rarely met in direct competition, the Finn having progressed through

New team, new vehicle for 1996. But first the Marlboro McLaren Mercedes F1 ski week and a race round Madonna di Campiglio on a ski-doo (McLaren).

the junior formulae a year earlier than Coulthard, head to head with another Scot, Allan McNish.

Also a factor in play for McLaren at the beginning of 1996 was that four times World Champion Alain Prost had been brought in to try to make the team competitive. Prost had been hired the previous season by Ron Dennis who, inexplicably, failed to inform sponsors Marlboro of the move – an oversight that would lead directly to the cigarette company transferring its money to Ferrari for 1997. The Frenchman had been out of racing for a year (and would, at the end of the season, purchase the Ligier team to race under the Prost banner in 1997) but he was still a quick driver. Formidably quick according to Coulthard who first experienced Prost at Estoril in February when the revised McLaren made its debut. The new car was, according to Coulthard mimicking Prost at this first test, 'zee dog's knob' and certainly in the limited amount of pre-season testing it appeared to be just that, topping the final test times at Estoril before the cars were flown out to Australia for the first race of the 1996 season.

But testing is one thing, the white heat of a race weekend something else again. No-one really knows what car is going to be fastest until they compete in earnest. In 1996 it was the Williams Renault, yet again. Lack of grip and balance affected both McLarens at Melbourne. Hakkinen, with more experience of the twitchy chassis, qualified fifth. Coulthard, his confidence shaken by a car which, compared with the Williams, seemed almost unbelievable, was a lowly 13th, nearly one and a half seconds off the pace.

In the race it hardly mattered. Going into the first corner Jordan driver Rubens Barrichello moved over on Olivier Panis in the Ligier who braked. Coulthard, coming hard, swerved across the track into Johnny Herbert's Sauber. Martin Brundle, in the second Jordan, had nowhere to go and was launched into one of the most spectacular crashes of the season. Coulthard took the spare car for the restart but struggled for 24 laps until the throttle jammed.

In Brazil things seemed to have improved dramatically, with Hakkinen and Coulthard third and fourth respectively in the first, untimed practice. But it was an illusory showing. Hakkinen qualified seventh, the Scot 14th. Race day brought rain, something that would

There's also the question of attaining the peak fitness required in today's F1 paddock (McLaren).

149

favour the less powerful cars but help the most driveable ones. The McLaren was neither.

At the start, however, something very interesting happened. Coulthard made up five places and by lap 19 had worked his way through the spray up to seventh spot on the slippery track. On lap 22, with the rain stopped and a dry line beginning to appear, Coulthard was the first driver in for slicks – but the rain had already restarted and he spun out of the race on lap 29. That could happen to anyone, however. Jacques Villeneuve, the new Williams wunderkind, had spun off three laps earlier. Mika Hakkinen struggled home fourth, just ahead of Salo in the Tyrrell. In Argentina McLaren's fortunes were no better. Coulthard, ninth on the grid, finished the race in seventh position; the Finn, starting from eighth position, retired on lap 19 with a dicey throttle valve.

Back in Europe, for the fourth round at Nurburgring, home ground for Mercedes-Benz, Coulthard finally outqualified his team-mate to put his car in sixth place for the start, three ahead of the Finn. Little surprise then that before the race he was in high spirits – but more was to come, for there was the arithmetic. In each race so far he had made up four places on the grid. If he did that again today he would go round the first corner in third. And if he held third until the end . . .

He did, to the delight of Mercedes-Benz personnel and the home crowd. Never mind Villeneuve and Schumacher fighting for first, or World Championship leader Damon Hill being relegated to fourth, the most impressive sight at the start of the 1996 European Grand Prix was the red and white Mercedes McLaren thundering down the inside into the first corner to take second place behind Villeneuve in the Williams.

Schumacher was briefly third, but that would not last. And that was basically the story of the race. Hakkinen, undoubtedly fired up by the sight of his 'junior' team-mate way out in front, incurred two separate stop/go penalties and finished nowhere. Damon Hill, driving the best car in the world on a fast circuit, had to follow Coulthard home.

On the podium alongside Villeneuve enjoying his maiden win and Schumacher Ferrari's best result of the season, Coulthard looked happy, and relieved.

Right *Coulthard looked happy enough with the move* (McLaren).

Round five was the San Marino Grand Prix at Imola, perhaps the most atmospheric track on the calendar and, since the deaths there of Ayrton Senna and Roland Ratzenberger two years before, certainly the most poignant. Coulthard qualified fourth, and everyone rechecked their arithmetic. Fourteenth to ninth in Brazil, ninth to fifth in Argentina, sixth to second in Germany, fourth to . . ? No, no way. That sort of thing simply does not happen.

It did. A McLaren led the pack out of the first corner for the first time since Senna's reign. For 19 glorious laps, until the first of two pit stops, Coulthard in the McLaren, led a Grand Prix on merit.

But now Schumacher, with a clear track ahead, put in two blinding laps so that he could come out ahead of Coulthard. This is an old Schuey trick and it worked. Damon Hill, on one stop, took the lead and held it and that's how they finished. Coulthard retired on lap 44, dicey gearbox hydraulics. Hakkinen, out with engine problems, had got

But everyone acknowledged that after his debut seasons at Williams driving the best car in Formula 1, the sweat and toil would now begin in earnest (McLaren).

another stop/go penalty, this time for ignoring the blue flag hung out to warn drivers that they are about to be overtaken by faster traffic.

Monaco was simply madness. Schumacher smashed into the wall on the opening lap, Hill's engine blew when he was miles in the lead. Alesi's car fell apart under him, Irvine crashed and took off three more. In the end there were only three cars running – Panis, then Coulthard, with Herbert a distant third. Panis had passed the Scot in the pits, but out on the track, though Coulthard could get up to the Ligier, he could not find a way by. Second in these conditions was good enough.'I was hoping that Olivier might make a mistake,' said Coulthard. 'But I drove against him in Formula 3000, and I know he does not make mistakes.' (In a way though it was fortunate that the Scot did not score his maiden victory for McLaren Mercedes at this, the most famous track in motor racing. In the wet conditions before the race he had

Coulthard had some excellent advisers in engineer David Brown (left) and four times World Champion Alain Prost (McLaren).

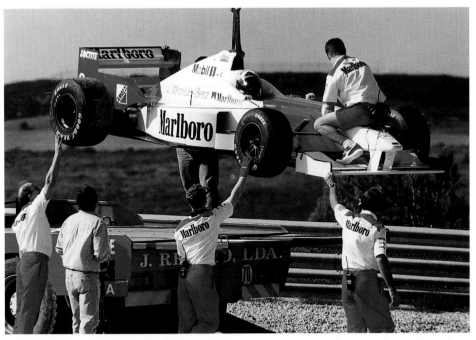

But although Coulthard gave McLaren their best result, a second at Monaco, it wasn't to be a successful season. All up in the air seems to sum up 1996 for the flying Scot (Empics).

found his helmet misting badly and so had borrowed Schumacher's spare. Made by the same company, this was roughly the same size. The German's colours would have raised some eyebrows however.)

If the McLaren team in general and Coulthard in particular went to Spain with high hopes they were to be sadly disappointed. Neither driver could get the car to handle anything like half decently and the times showed it – Hakkinen 2.5 seconds off the pace, Coulthard nearly three. The race was wet, very wet. Coulthard hit a car at the start and knocked a complete front corner off the McLaren. He still does not know who or what he hit. Hakkinen dragged the surviving car home in fifth place.

Canada was simply hard work. Coulthard slugged home fourth, Hakkinen fifth. It was World Championship points in the bag, Scot beats Finn. France was little better though Hakkinen, for some strange reason, arrived hinting at victory. In the warm-up Hakkinen was third, Coulthard fourth. The race was another hard slog to fifth and sixth, particularly for Coulthard who fumbled his start and had to follow

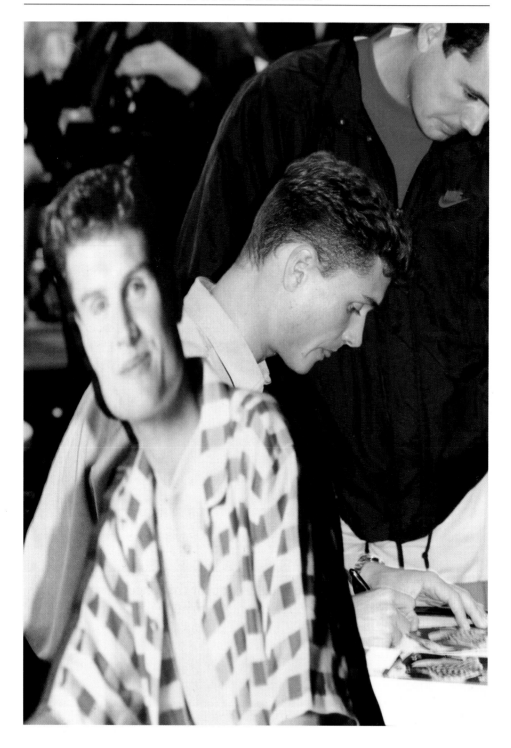

Left Small wonder he was in two minds that year about his chances of regaining the performance he had enjoyed with Williams (The Scotsman).

Brundle's Jordan until the first round of pit stops. Still, at least they fared better than pole man Schumacher. His engine exploded on the parade lap. The British Grand Prix at Silverstone was a re-run. Hakkinen and Coulthard were bit players, struggling home third and fifth.

Hockenheim could and should have been different. After all it was a home track for Mercedes and the lap record belonged to Coulthard. Hakkinen could only qualify fourth, with Coulthard seventh despite the Scot being by far the fastest car on the track, breaking the speed trap at 221.897 mph. In the warm-up they were first and second but in the race, running full fuel loads, the McLarens simply could not get round the fast corners. Coulthard finished fifth, Hakkinen retired when his gearbox broke 13 laps into the race.

On the tight and twisty Hungaroring neither driver expected much. Hakkinen finished fourth, Coulthard lasted until lap 23 when the engine blew. For the Scot, Hungary proved to be the story of the rest of the season – no points despite all the effort.

Hakkinen, by contrast finished third in Belgium, Italy and Japan to score 12 championship points. Not that they really mattered however for at the end of a dismal season McLaren finished a distant fourth in the constructor's championship (49 points, against Williams-Renault's 175), but it was easily the best of the rest with more than twice the number of points scored by fifth placed Jordan (22). In the driver's championship, won by Damon Hill with 97 points, Hakkinen was a distant fifth (31) with Coulthard (18) in seventh place behind Berger (21). Although they had led races and on at least a couple of occasions come close to winning, McLaren Mercedes finished the year as also-rans. It simply was not good enough – not for this once illustrious team, not for Mercedes-Benz and certainly not for the flying Scot.

• APPENDIX •

David Coulthard's career highlights

1983/5
Scottish Junior Kart Champion in 1983, 1984 and 1985

1986/7
Scottish Open and British Super 1 Kart Champion

1988
Scottish Open Kart Champion

1989
Winner of both single seater Junior FF1600 Championships

1990
Fourth in British Vauxhall Lotus challenge and fifth in GM Lotus Euroseries (despite a broken leg)
First Grand Prix Car Drive: 1990 Silverstone McLaren-Honda (prize for winning the McLaren-*Autosport* Young Driver of the Year Award)

1991
Second in British Formula 3 Championship including five wins

1992
Ninth in the European Formula 3000 Championship
Tested with Camel Benetton Ford Formula 1 team

1993
Third in the Formula 3000 Championship
Tested the Williams Renault FW15C
Won the GT Class of the Le Mans 24 Hour Race for Jaguar

1994
Formula 1, Williams Renault
Spanish GP: Qualified ninth, retired (electrics)
Canadian GP: Qualified fifth, finished fifth
British GP: Qualified seventh, finished fifth
German GP: Qualified sixth, fastest lap, retired (electrics)
Hungarian GP: Qualified third, crashed
Belgian GP: Qualified seventh, finished fourth
Italian GP: Qualified fifth, finished sixth (ran out of fuel)
Portuguese GP: Qualified third, finished second, fastest lap
F3000 Silverstone: Qualified third, finished second

1995

Williams Renault

Brazilian GP: Qualified third, finished second

Argentinian Grand Prix: Pole, retired (throttle)

San Marino GP: Qualified third, finished fourth

Spanish GP: Qualified fourth, retired (gearbox)

Monaco GP: Qualified third, retired (throttle/gearbox)

Canadian GP: Qualified third, spun

French GP: Qualified third, finished third

British GP: Qualified third, finished third

German GP: Qualified third, finished second

Hungarian GP: Qualified second, finished second

Belgian GP: Qualified fifth, fastest lap, retired (gearbox)

Italian GP: Pole: crashed

Portuguese GP: Pole, won, fastest lap

European GP: Pole, finished third

Pacific GP: Pole, finished second

Japanese GP: Qualified sixth, crashed

Australian GP: Qualified second, crashed

1996

McLaren Mercedes

Australian GP: Qualified 13th, retired (stuck throttle)

Brazilian GP: Qualified fourteenth, spun

Argentinian GP: Qualified ninth, finished seventh

European GP: Qualified sixth, finished third

San Marino: Qualified fourth, retired (gearbox hydraulics)

Monaco GP: Qualified fifth, finished second

Spanish GP: Qualified fourteenth, crashed

Canadian GP: Qualified tenth, finished fourth

French GP: Qualified seventh, finished sixth

British GP: Qualified ninth, finished fifth

German GP: Qualified seventh, finished fifth

Hungarian GP: Qualified ninth, retired (engine)

Belgian GP: Qualified fourth, spun

Italian GP: Qualified fifth, crashed

Portuguese GP: Qualified eighth, finished 13th

Japanese GP: Qualified eighth, finished eighth

1997

McLaren Mercedes

Australian GP: Qualified fourth, won

Brazilian GP: Qualified twelfth, finished tenth

Argentinian GP: Qualified tenth, crashed

San Marino GP: Qualified tenth, retired (engine)

Monaco GP: Qualified fifth, crashed

Spanish GP: Qualified third, finished sixth